FEATHERS ARE EVERYWHERE

A Practical Application of the
Law of Attraction

Randy Nathan, MA, MSW

PNG Publishing, 19 Stone Drive, West Orange, NJ 07052
A Your Personal Coach, LLC Department
www.ProjectNextGen.com

Printed in the United States of America

*PNG Publishing and the author disclaim responsibility for adverse
effects or consequences from the misapplication or injudicious use of
information contained in the book. Mention of resources and
associations does not imply endorsement by PNG Publishing or the
author.*

ISBN-13: 978-0-9992911-7-7

DEDICATION

~ To Mikayla and Brianna ~
For your tenacity, love,
and incredible souls.

Thank you for being born to me!

Skyler,

MAY THE WORDS HERE IN
PROVIDE MOTIVATION, SUPPORT
& GUIDANCE.
FEATHERS ARE EVERYWHERE!

Warmly,
Coort

TABLE OF CONTENTS

INTRODUCTION

"When feathers appear, angels are near."
Author Unknown

Feathers are vital to a birds survival. They help birds fly, keep them warm, provide protection from nature's elements, and serve as camouflage from predators. With over 10,000 different types of birds, feathers are as colorful as they are unique. They are everywhere.

Birds primarily loose feathers during a process called molting. Depending on the species, it can occur only once or at various times shedding old feathers with the new. As the feathers detach, gravity pulls them to the ground.

What happens when you stumble across a feather on your path? What does it mean to you?

The ancient Egyptians believed feathers were a symbol of the Goddess of Truth, Justice, and Order. While Native Americans believe that feathers carry stories, mystical meaning and even magic. In the Bible, feathers represent loving care, protection, and a symbol of dreams. In those dreams, feathers often suggest wealth and riches, or undertaking a journey. Feathers are also spirituality connected. For some, finding a feather is a magical moment transcending time connecting consciousness to a higher spirit. Regardless of your belief, there is no doubt you have seen a feather or two.

INTRODUCTION

Feathers can represent how the universe sends us signs. Since life has ups and downs, twists and turns, and is often unpredictable, it is essential to develop strategies to provide meaning during the difficult times. It is easy to live when life provides riches, rewards and wealth. However, it is when the "going gets tough" that requires vital survival skills to keep moving forward.

What if seeing a feather was truly magical? What if it really was the universe providing support, guidance and love? What if feathers are sent your way to comfort you and encourage you along your path? Feathers have a connection to birds, and birds have wings. Wings are a symbol of flight, and angels have wings. Angels soar above us, looking at things from a different perspective. They know that you can move beyond all limitations.

Being Happy

It seems nearly everyone has a negative attitude. People either act like a victim of their circumstances or live with significant feelings of conflict. If we are not feeling sorry for ourselves, we are angry with others for what occurs in our life. How can it be that so many are not able to achieve what they desire most? Why does happiness seem so elusive?

INTRODUCTION

The truth is, most people are not taught correctly about happiness. They are trained that happiness is a result of certain actions. Happiness is achieved by following appropriate steps. Do "A" and "B" then happiness will be attained. There is a presumed "blueprint" that originates in middle school ~ study hard, get good grades, get into a good college, get a good job, make a lot of money, and be *happy*. To be *happy*, one must accomplish these various steps with happiness being the outcome. It is so ingrained in us that any steps that deviate from this "blueprint" may create just the opposite of happiness. And, that result is not acceptable.

The Opposite of Happy

What is the opposite of happy? Sad? Not true. The opposite of happy is ~ not happy. Napoleon Hill[1] often said, "The only thing that has meaning, is the meaning you give to things." Even though being "not happy" can mean a number of different feelings, the belief is that sadness is the opposite and must be avoided. Being sad is bad. It is an emotion that must be evaded at all costs. In Disney's Pixar movie (2015), "*Inside-Out*" this desire plays out in a perfect example. Without spoiling the plot, throughout the movie there is constant drive to keep sadness away without interfering in life. However, the harder the characters try to keep sadness away, the more

INTRODUCTION

invasive it becomes. It is a perfect metaphor for life. The more we focus on not being happy the more it seems to be relevant. It appears that no matter what transpires a constant stream of unhappiness is present with an inability to be happy as the consequence.

*What would give for an entire year's worth
of happiness?*

Let's assume that you will receive 365 days of continued happiness upon conclusion of this book. How would you know at day 217 that you are truly "happy?" The answer may seem obvious as the most common response is often, "I'm happy because that's the way I would feel." Yet, by day 217, there is really no way to know if you would be truly "happy." The only way to feel happy is to have something to compare it to in that moment. One must experience being unhappy to gauge their level of happiness. And, accordingly, the only way to experience being unhappy is to know what it feels like to be happy. The opposites coexist for us to appreciate both feelings. No one can ever be happy without also being unhappy.

The Millennial's Pursuit for Being Happy

The generation currently impacted the most in this search for happiness is the Millennial generation. These are the youngest identified generation born

INTRODUCTION

between 1980 and 2001. They have grown up in a tech savvy environment, raised by 'helicopter' and 'snowplow' parents, with happiness being the ultimate reward.

A 2014 study administered by Allidura, GSW and The Harris Poll surveyed over 3500 Millennials, Gen Xers, and Baby Boomers.[3] Millennials are considered by many experts to be the first generation to deal with challenges primarily through data and technology. The most significant life-defining events that have shaped the Millennial generation are the shootings at Columbine High School, 9/11 Terrorist Attacks, Corporate scandals, the War on Drugs and the War on Terror. These moments in history have played a significant role in their overall goals and life experiences. Throughout childhood, their parents have played a very "hands-on" role, yet have done so from a substantial distance. Since the cost of living has increased so substantially throughout the country, Millennials are the first generation to be raised by support providers other than their parents, or other family members. Most were raised by day care centers, babysitters, nannies, and other care givers.

A main focus for parents of these Millennials is a desire for their children to be successful and happy. With that, parents went out of their way to provide life experiences to ensure their children's

INTRODUCTION

happiness. The outcome is that nearly 97% of Millennials say that being happy is important to them.[3] However, what is most interesting is just how disconnected this generation is in terms of what happiness truly is and how it can be achieved.

A History Lesson

Viktor Frankl was a prominent psychiatrist and neurologist living in Vienna in 1942. He was arrested and transported to a Nazi concentration camp with his wife and parents. Three years later, following the liberation of his camp, most of his family, including his pregnant wife were dead. His prisoner number ***119104*** was permanently embedded in his arm as a reminder of what was forever taken from him.

Within a year of leaving the camp (1946), Frankl published one of the top ten most influential books in American history, *Man's Search for Meaning*.[4] He wrote about his experience in the camp in nine days and concluded that the primary difference between those individuals who survived compared to those that did not came down to one basic thing: *meaning*. The prisoners that were able to find meaning in the most horrendous of life experiences were more resilient than those that could not. Frankl wrote, "Everything can be taken from a man but one thing, the last of the human freedoms -- to choose one's attitude in any given set of circumstances, to choose one's own way.[4]" You can only control your attitude and your effort. However, many seem to have difficulties with their overall attitude. Since so much meaning is directed towards happiness, it often becomes an obsessive march towards an expected outcome. Then, even when the outcome is favorable, the feeling of happiness is often evasive. Therein, lies one of the largest challenges of human life.

Feathers are Everywhere

Although this book is not specifically about being happy, it is about the symbolism of feathers and finding happiness as a byproduct of what occurs all around us. Most individuals experience happiness as a result of some type of achievement, or goal (witness the Millennials). Happiness is only experienced when something goes right. The formula for this is:

If I get A, then B happens
If I do not get A, then I do not get B
A = Goal/Achievement/Money
B = Happiness

It is a formula that is instilled in most people at a very early age. It is a process that gets reinforced through our schools, parenting, athletics, work

INTRODUCTION

environment, and so on. However, this process is no longer sufficient. It is no longer the way life has to be viewed. Whether it is through quantum physics, Law of Attraction, Positive Psychology, or other alternatives that focus on happiness, goals and achievement, information (both through research and opinions) is available that proves and demonstrates that happiness is a state of being, not a result of a life's occurrences.

Happiness really is all around us, even in the most difficult of times and the darkest of days. Feathers remind us there is a silver lining. It takes understanding, certain skills, and a little bit of faith to help most individuals see that on a daily basis. This book is designed to provide a basic and simple understanding of the Law of Attraction (LOA), identify unique skills to incorporate the LOA, and introduce a number of principles that can be utilized immediately.

Just like happiness is a state of being and is all around us, feathers are everywhere, both literally and figuratively. It is just a matter of awareness and being able to see them in every day life. I encourage you to test out this concept. The idea is to "attract" a feather into your life. Be open to the idea at some point in the next few days, you will see a random feather. It will present itself, but you must be willing to be open to the idea that it is

INTRODUCTION

possible. All you have to do is look and it will appear. Once you start attracting feathers, your mantra will become "Feathers Are Everywhere." However, it really is a metaphor that represents so many items relevant to life. Whether its happiness, money, love, kindness, or good health all that needs to be done is look around and notice how it already is within every element of life. Happiness is everywhere; money is everywhere; love is everywhere!

THE LAW OF ATTRACTION

"If you will it, it is no dream."
Theodore Herzl

The "Law of Attraction" was first introduced to me at the beginning of my professional coach training. I was halfway through my education when one of my classmates shared the concept with me. I was very skeptical at first. It was easy to understand how it worked for achieving goals and positive life experiences, but there was difficulty with how it operated when challenges and struggles occurred. Grasping the knowledge that a person **attracts** bad things was extremely problematic. Why would anyone knowingly want to have bad things happen in life?

"Murphy's Law"

Many years ago when life was extremely challenging I was driving to Lake Ontario to spend the weekend salmon fishing with an old friend. Approximately four hours into the drive, as my friend and I were talking, a rock flew into my windshield. Fortunately it didn't shatter the glass, but it created a serious crack that would need to be fixed. It felt like it fell from the sky. I was driving north on a two-lane highway, in the middle of the day, no other cars were within miles and there wasn't a cloud in the sky. Yet, somehow my car was struck by a rock.

14

THE LAW OF ATTRACTION

How could that be? I took it as a warning. I started screaming at the sky as loud as I could. Yelling at whoever or whatever would be listening to come and get me, it was a challenge. I was waiting for him (or it) to smite me; daring him to create further harm. My friend speaks of this with a great sense of humor, but at the time I think it freaked him out. I was mad and tired of life being so awful. I was done with being a target of life's events. My life was Murphy's Law, "Whatever could go wrong, would go wrong...to me." It was just my luck that my car would be struck by a rock at that moment and at that time. If I was standing outside and birds flew by, I would be the one with bird excrement on my head. I'm the one that bad things happened to.

The trip to Lake Ontario demonstrates how the Law of Attraction works. Even though I didn't want bad things to happen to me, my energy and thoughts were focused on everything bad that was happening. In essence, I attracted the rock into my window.

In simplest terms, the "Law of Attraction" (LOA) states that what you think about you bring about. When thoughts are optimistic, positive things

THE LAW OF ATTRACTION

transpire. When thoughts are negative, undesirable things happen. It seems easy, yet challenges rational thought. That's why it was so puzzling for me to wrap my head around the "Law of Attraction." I didn't want bad things to happen to me, yet they were. How could I be responsible for the bad things happening in my life? It seemed preposterous.

There are a number of national experts that are able to provide greater insight into the "Law of Attraction." Napoleon Hill is the author of "Think and Grow Rich" (1932), Michael Losier[5] is the author of "Law of Attraction: The Science of Attracting More of What You Want and Less of What You Don't Want" (2003), Esther and Jerry Hicks[6] are the authors of "Ask and It Is Given: Learning to Manifest Your Desires" (2004) and channels "The Teachings of Abraham," and Rhonda Byrne[7] is the author of the highly admired book, "The Secret" (2006). They are the true experts and I encourage you to read more from them. They all explain the power of LOA and how to best utilize your energy and vibrations.

The LOA is a three-step method, using the acronym D.B.A. ~ Desire, Belief and Accept. The more renowned experts focus on energy and the vibrations that a person sends out into the universe. It resonates with me but most people struggle to understand. Its like "karma" ~ what goes around

THE LAW OF ATTRACTION

comes round. Even though energy exists everywhere and in everything, most individuals have trouble accepting it because it makes them uncomfortable. LOA, energy, and vibrations are "out there" for the "average" person. Unfortunately not everyone is open to these ideas.

In order to see "Feathers are Everywhere" it is important to have a general appreciation about the basic tenets of the LOA. There are two fundamental types of energy/vibrations ~ positive and negative. Each person is made up of energy with vibrations being sent out to the world. A significant portion of LOA has to do with the unintentional factors that are being transmitted, not necessarily the thoughts/ feelings in the conscious realm. Therefore a person may have logical thoughts of happiness, but deep within their own psyche there is self-doubt and worthlessness. They have a powerful inner voice that is self-deprecating. This immense negative thinking contradicts the positive thoughts, thereby "attracting" the unwanted situation. If an external action is to achieve some type of goal, a person may have a negative inner thought that says, "I'm not good enough and never will be." Even though the external action is focused on the wanted result, the internal energy vibrating out to the universe attracts a negative outcome. The subconscious thoughts override the conscious thinking.

THE LAW OF ATTRACTION

"The Law of Gravity"

For the "doubters," the most effective way to grasp LOA is by examining the science behind gravity. Gravity is an abstract theory that nearly all people take for granted. Not much thought is given as to how it works and why. We accept the notion called gravity because we do not float in the air. Therefore gravity is real and works. There are two schools of thought regarding gravity-one is "Newton's Law of Gravity" the other is "Einstein's Theory of Relatively." Each school of thought has been researched, argued, and promoted as being the best explanation for how gravity works. Yet, regardless of the interpretation, there is universal agreement that gravity exists.

We may not know how gravity works, but we certainly know that it does. Surprisingly, the Law Of Attraction operates in a similar manner. Meaning, LOA occurs whether you know how or not. One does not "need" to know how it works, other than to accept that it does. Whether you want to accept that LOA is present in daily life is ultimately up to you. Even though there is no scientific equation, it does exist.

When the Law of Attraction was first introduced to me, it was taught using the acronym DBA. "D" was a Desire to achieve; "B" was a Belief that you deserve that achievement; and "A" was an

THE LAW OF ATTRACTION

Acceptance that the achievement was already happening. The term "live as if" was the phrase that was used to implement the formula. Other phrases used are "fake it, until you make it," or "dress for the position you want to have." These are all references to the powerful uses of the Law of Attraction. Ideally, a person that subscribes to the LOA understands that they have the ability to manifest whatever aspirations they have in life. It is relatively easy to maintain the desire to gain what you really want.

THE THREE STEPS

"Do. Or do not. There is no try."
Yoda (Jedi Master)

The Law of Attraction states that we attract into our lives whatever we give our attention, energy and focus to, whether we want it or not. What you bring into your life is a result of what you think- consciously and subconsciously. If your thoughts are about success, good things and feeling good, then that is what you get. But, if you have negative thoughts, focus on bad memories or worry about things, then that is exactly what is going to happen to you. Its like hitting every red light when you are in a rush.

This law is very difficult for most people to understand and live by. For obvious reasons, we don't want bad things to happen to us. We want happiness, peace and success. However, in reality, we often don't get the grades we want, or the job, or the friends, or… It goes on and on and on. It is difficult for us to accept that what we lack is the direct result of our own thoughts, energy and focus. Therefore, we often believe there are external limitations, causes or sources that create our challenges and problems. Why would we want to have bad or unpleasant things happen to us? It is too painful to accept that we are responsible for what happens to us and much easier to place blame on outside sources. However, a person who

THE THREE STEPS

lives by the Law of Attraction knows this is not the case!

I encourage a three-step structure that may resonate easier than the DBA. It allows the client to accept the method more willingly. The three steps are ~ Be Clear, Remove Obstacles, and Focus (& Refocus). It is only after an opportunity to use these three steps that a person is open to the higher level of learning with the LOA. A person must first "see" how it works. Regardless of the individual, this approach offers a left-brain strategy (logic) allowing right brain thinking (creative).

> **Step 1 - Be Extremely Clear**

> **Step 2 - Remove Obstacles**

> **Step 3 - Focus (& Refocus)**

With any goal, it is very important to clearly express your wants. The clearer you are about what you want, the greater the opportunities to succeed. Next it is vital to identify and remove the various obstacles (both internal and external). The people who understand that obstacles are part of the learning process will embrace adversity instead of

THE THREE STEPS

placing blame. Finally, even though some obstacles are identified, there will be unexpected challenges to achieving the goal resulting in the need to refocus. If setting and achieving goals was easy, then everyone would do it. However, most people get discouraged and stop chasing their dreams because they are not able to overcome their challenges. It is easier to give up, then fight for what they really want.

Step One – Be Extremely Clear

When I teach LOA and coach my clients, I utilize a distinct approach. Since most of my clients are Millennials, business executives, or athletes, I have had to adapt this concept to a manner in which they are more open to absorb this message. When I first introduce the idea, I often have to ask them to simply listen and not judge. Prior to sharing my approach, I ask them to identify three to five things out of their control. Then after some dialogue, I ask the to identify the two main factors within their control–their attitude and their effort. They are the only items within anyone's power. If they are willing to give me their best attitude and greatest effort, it increases the learning curve. Then I ask them what is the first thing that must be decided when going on vacation?

THE THREE STEPS

Vacations

When was the last time you went on vacation? As a sole proprietor and entrepreneur, the opportunity for vacations are rare. However, when it is time for a vacation I get euphoric. Research supports that Americans are most likely to waste a majority of their acquired vacation time. However, getting away for vacations is essential in revitalizing and refocusing. We all need a break from the "rat race" of life.

So, what does going on vacation and "Feathers" have to do with one another?

Once it has been decided that there is a need to get away, what's the first decision that must be made? How do you go about the process of going on a vacation? What's the first move?

The first step is to figure out the destination. Once that is determined, steps can be made to ensure a wonderful vacation. To know how to get to your location, what to pack, and what you are going to do, the first step is to pick an endpoint. Then everything falls into place. To attract "Feathers" the first step is to know where you are headed.

There are three vital questions that must be answered to know what you really want. The first question is, *"Who are you?"* Ironically, that is one

THE THREE STEPS

of the most difficult questions for people to answer. The common response is a name, a gender, and job title, but that is not necessarily who you really are. The second question is, *"Where are you going?"* That's a bit easier, since it involves an element of action and provides some type of direction. This question is essential as it allows the person to focus on being extremely clear on what he/she really wants. The third and final question is, *"How are you going to get there?"* This is the action plan that will guide you into getting what it is that you really want. However, there are usually challenges and obstacles that arise as you head towards your desired goal. How you deal with adversity and challenges is an essential component in your journey. Most people get frustrated; blame their external environment and give up on their dream.

Your inner Cheerleader

Close your eyes and imagine that you live in a magical place. It is a world where dreams come true and you get what you want most in your life. You see the people in your life that love and support you most. They are jumping up and down, encouraging you, motivating you and screaming their support. You feel safe, secure and know deep within yourself that anything you want is achievable. This special place is open to any idea,

---

THE THREE STEPS

opportunity or dream. However, your ideas must be extremely precise. If you are not specific, or have any doubt, then it will fade away. Once you are certain about what you want, you can develop a well organized plan, identify opportunities to help you achieve what you want, and remove the obstacles that are in your way.

To help know what you want, it is also important to identify what you don't want. Take a few moments and write down what you do not want in your life at this moment (a particular job you don't want, a particular way of live you no longer want, a habit you no longer want, etc.)

List what you don't want
1
2
3
4
5

THE THREE STEPS

Next, list what you do want. When you think of success, what does that mean? What awaits you and your dreams? What are your personal and professional goals? What matters most in your life? The clearer you are, the better!

List what you do want
1
2
3
4
5

Now, write a detailed *statement* about what you want. Be as clear and direct as possible. When you accurately identify what you want you can then visualize what it will be like when you have it.

THE THREE STEPS

What I want:

Step Two – Remove the Obstacles

For step one to work effectively, step two is essential. Removing the obstacles is critical in achieving what you really want. Obstacles are the elements that interfere with achieving goals. Most individuals do not have the determination or commitment to overcome these challenges. Adversity stops them the moment it arises. They believe the challenge is external and "out of their control." They become victims of their own circumstances blaming their situation on others. They feel sorry for themselves, they curse and yell, and they take their frustrations out on those

THE THREE STEPS

individuals around them. They feel that life is happening to them making matters worse. They don't realize that life's most difficult challenges are really an internal process.

The Paradigm Shift

Starting at an early age, we are conditioned to avoid sadness, failure and making mistakes. Our parents do everything within their power to help us avoid the unpleasant emotions that come with those experiences. They become "snow plows," removing challenges and difficulties. Or, they become "helicopters" hovering to protect from adversity.

Parents, schools, and the media all promote that happiness is a byproduct of what happens in life. It is a result of something occurring, not a state of being. It is an achievement to be accomplished. It is only later in life that we are open to a different understanding of happiness. Maybe it's a life crisis, Near Death Experience, or an unexpected loss of a loved one that forces us to reevaluate our life in that moment. Life provides a literal shift in our thinking from that point forward.

The concept of a paradigm shift is a scientific term. In the early 1960s, Thomas Kuhn defined it as a "series of peaceful interludes punctuated, by intellectually violent revolutions" causing "one

THE THREE STEPS

conceptual world view to be replaced by another view." Basically, a paradigm shift occurs when a significant change happens-usually from one fundamental view to another. It represents the notion of a major change in a certain thought or change in personal beliefs, systems or organizations. This new view replaces the former way of thinking. Thereby allowing the person a choice in which perspective makes the most sense at that time.

A Paradigm Shift:
The Story of King Solomon

One day King Solomon decided to humble his most trusted servant. The other servants were overly jealous and he needed to be humbled. He said to him, "There is a certain ring that I want you to bring to me. I wish to wear it for the next festival, which gives you six months to find it."

"If it exists anywhere on earth, your majesty," replied the servant, "I will find it and bring it to you, but what makes the ring so special?"

"It has special powers," answered the king. "If a man looks at it and he is happy, he becomes sad, and if a sad man looks at it, he becomes happy." Solomon knew that no

---

THE THREE STEPS

such ring existed in the world, but he wished to give his servant some added humility.

Spring passed and then summer, and still the servant had no idea where he could find the ring. On the day before the festival, he decided to take a walk in one of the poorest quarters of town. He passed by a merchant who had begun to set out the day's wares on a shabby carpet. "Have you by any chance heard of a special ring that makes the happy wearer forget his joy and the broken-hearted wearer forget his sorrows?" asked the servant. "I'm looking for it for the king."

He watched the elderly man take a plain gold ring from his carpet and engrave something on it. When he was finished he placed it into a box to be given to the king.

That night the entire city welcomed in the festival with great excitement "Well," said King Solomon to the servant, "have you found what I sent you after?" All the other servants laughed as he walked shaking towards the king.

To everyone's surprise, the servant held up a small box and with his voice shaking declared, "Here it is, your majesty!" The

THE THREE STEPS

king grabbed the box and immediately opened it up. As soon as Solomon read the inscription on the ring, the smile vanished from his face. When he looked back at the ring, the smile return. Everyone in attendance stood in shocked silence.

The jeweler had transcribed four words on the gold band: "This too shall pass." At that moment Solomon realized that all his wisdom and fabulous wealth and tremendous power were fleeting things, for one day he would be nothing but dust. Then looking at the ring again, he realized everything that he had created and the gratitude that existed and he was pleased.

What do you see in the picture below?

THE THREE STEPS

The image that most individuals see is a left profile of a person (eyes, nose, mouth and neck). However, if you slowly turn the book to the left, your perspective will change. It is now possible to see the word "Liar" written in cursive at an angle. Or, maybe you initially viewed the word first, then by shifting the book you now see the profile. By a simple twist of the wrist, what you see changes. The image stays the same, but your perspective changes.

A paradigm is a person's habits and behavior. Your thoughts, ideas, choices and actions are an accumulation of your previous life experiences, learning, and routines. These habits are imbedded within you. They drive your internal choices whether consciously or subconsciously. In this realm, a paradigm shift is a personal revolution in how one views their own reality. It renders old perceptions and beliefs false and no longer viable, opening a completely new way of being and thinking.

Here's another example-Imagine you are holding a new baseball in your hand. It's white, with red stitches. Then you put on blue tinted glasses. The color of the ball becomes blue. A similar change occurs when a pair of rose tinted glasses are worn. The ball appears pink. When the glasses are removed the color of the ball is white again.

THE THREE STEPS

The color of the ball does not change. The color changes because of the different colored glasses. The lenses allow you to change your perspective.

Man and the Moon

On May 25th, 1961, President John F. Kennedy (JFK) announced to a special joint session of Congress that the United States would put a man on the moon by the end of the decade. Many throughout the world thought it was impossible but, JFK, LBJ and NASA knew otherwise. The doubters joked, "If God meant for man to fly he would have given us wings." However, only eight years later in 1969, a human being did walk on the moon defying all of the skeptics. A common expression from that became "if we can put a man on the moon, then we can do...." It became the rallying battle cry to create change by challenging the current beliefs and norms.

This same idea can occur within your life. You have the ability to perceive the life you want by changing your paradigm. By altering your thoughts, you can impact your feelings, thereby transforming your actions. Being able to view challenges with a different set of "lenses" allows you to appreciate the circumstances that present themselves. Being open

THE THREE STEPS

to a more positive perspective can change into a learning opportunity.

Using the glasses metaphor again, there is a saying, "Hindsight is 20/20." Meaning that if you had the ability to relive certain life experiences different outcomes would occur. Knowing what *did* happen allows you to better prepare and plan for those bad circumstances. Yet, the only reason why you learned how to deal with those negative outcomes, is the fact that you had to overcome them in the first place. Avoiding failure and mistakes in the long run, is actually more hurtful than helpful. Sure the experience in the moment may be painful, but the learning that comes from that event is extremely valuable in overcoming similar situations in the future.

Life happens in the present and comes at us quicker than expected. There are many people that seem to only be able to focus on the past, they dwell in it. The only good that can come from reflecting on the past, are those life lessons that make us bigger, better and stronger.

Those that live life looking through a rearview mirror often complain about things that already happened, find themselves a victim of their circumstances, and having significant difficulties overcoming obstacles. They dwell on those situations, hold grudges against others, and do not

THE THREE STEPS

allow themselves freedom from their thoughts. They are very unhappy people, making those around them just as miserable.

Experts often claim that the past cannot be changed. The past is in the past. Yet, that is not 100% truthful. Sure, one cannot change the actions that occurred in the past, but one can reshape their view, perspective, and understanding of what happened. If the lenses you choose to wear look at a past experience as bad, negative and hurtful, then the past is just that. However, if you allow yourself to change those lenses with a new more positive perspective, you can ask yourself, what was the lesson, what did I learn, how can I be better because of what transpired? There are no mistakes, there is no failure, just opportunities for growth.

Parrot, Limiting Beliefs & Perception (PLP)

There are a number of components in life creating a foundation that formats our thoughts, feelings and actions. There are biological, physiological, psychological, and sociological explanations that identify personality, behavior, and health. In addition, there are religious, cultural, socio-economic, and gender related impacts as well. There are thousands of experts all preaching their knowledge on life circumstances. Depending on where you live, who you are born to, what people

THE THREE STEPS

are involved with your life, there are many ways to get through life. Everyone has an opinion.

These external factors effect our life experiences numerous ways. Most importantly they impact our thoughts and beliefs, and influence the choices we make. In addition, given the multi-faceted media driven society in which we live, we are forced to consume pictures, advertisements, movies and numerous other images that dictate what life is supposed to look like, be and feel. We take all of those outside messages and formulate thoughts and feelings around those, creating a fictional perspective of what life is supposed to be. It becomes a reality based on our own perceptual illusion. We also have an internal voice that is based in fear that wants to protect us. It sits on our shoulder, murmuring "you're not good enough, no one likes you, don't even bother trying."

When faced with various life decisions we are confronted by the "BIG 3." These are the three main challenges that arise within our minds that stop us from accomplishing our dreams, or overcoming the necessary calculated risks to lead the types of lives we really want. The BIG 3 obstacles are an internal mechanism, regardless of those other external factors, that we each have stopping us from reaching our goals.

THE THREE STEPS

Parrot - Everyone has a Parrot that sits on his/her shoulder. The Parrot is the very powerful voice that repeats what it is told. It uses fear as its primary force to stop us from getting what we really want. The Parrot keeps us in our place by saying, "You're not good enough or You're not smart enough."

Limiting Beliefs - From the moment we are born we are taught and given beliefs that we transpose as truth. When choices in life arise, our beliefs impact what we choose to do. Limiting Beliefs are not necessarily right or wrong, good or bad. They simply are beliefs that may limit us from achieving our goals and reaching our fullest potential.

Perception - Our perception makes up our reality. Perception is our understanding of a situation and what is observed or thought. It is the culmination of our beliefs, life experiences, dreams and desires. Nothing is ever really as we perceive it to be, it's just an illusion to ourselves. (Remember the picture of the "man" a few pages ago? A slight twist of the page, and you saw the word "liar" instead.)

To get what you really want, addressing the BIG 3 allows you to acknowledge the internal negative blocks and validate their presence. Once you identify your BIG 3, you will no longer be held down. Achieving your goals is only a matter of understanding why your obstacles are present and what you can do within to remove them.

THE THREE STEPS

Here's how the BIG 3 work against you:

Putting Step 2 into Action

Close your eyes and identify those inner thoughts and feelings that tell you what you want is not possible (Think of The Big 3). Don't try to fight them, simply acknowledge them for being there. They are only trying to protect you. Now open your eyes and write down everything that you saw/heard in the tables below (1). Then fill-in the part of the table on what you will need to do to overcome them (2)—you may need to change your internal beliefs/attitudes or create external actions.

(1) Why you cannot achieve what you want
1
2
3
4
5

THE THREE STEPS

(2) What you need to do to overcome challenges
1
2
3
4
5

Once you clear the obstacles you will always take confident and consistent action towards that goal. You will focus on what you need to do (2) and not allow those items in (1) get in your way.

Step Three – Focus (& Refocus)

With a clear direction about what you want and having identified the obstacles, you can now focus on what it will take to get what you want. By centering on what you want you can think the necessary thoughts to reach your goal quicker and more effectively. It encourages you to overcome the challenges by enabling you to concentrate on where you are headed. Having a clear goal increases confidence that the plan will work. In addition, since there is an end goal, you can

THE THREE STEPS

visualize what it will feel and look like when you achieve it.

Geometry teaches that the shortest distance between two points is a straight line. Mathematically it is a formula that works every time. However, setting goals and achieving them is not that simple. If it were that easy to identify what you want with a clear path to get there, everyone would be doing it. Life does not provide a wide open direct line. Challenges and difficulties impact every single person. Obstacles in life do not discriminate. They do not care what color you are, live in a city or a suburb, are young or old, or are rich or poor. No matter what goal is established, at some point something will occur that will stand in the way of the plan. Maybe it is something expected, or possibly something that had not been considered. But something will happen to interfere, forcing you to hone in on your goal and focusing even harder.

Visualization

Many elite athletes utilize visualization to enhance their competitive edge. It is a technique that provides them with greater focus, determination and competitiveness. It is one of the most effective strategies in focusing on an end result, and allows an individual to "see" what it will take to overcome challenges and reach the finish line.

THE THREE STEPS

These world-class competitors understand the physical effort needed to compete at the highest level. However, nearly all would agree that mental preparation is also required. Many elite players highlight that the mental aspect is over 80% of their effort. Professional football players watch tape of past performances and their competition to better prepare themselves. Major League hitters watch video on opposing pitchers. They visualize their efforts using the new information.

Visualization allows the individual to create a mental image within their mind. This strategy provides a clear picture and impacts their "muscle memory." It enables the person to "visually" take the necessary physical steps to achieve their success. They see their effort play out in their mind. This mental exercise takes an abstract concept, thought or idea and creates a tangible hands on experience.

There are many benefits to visualization, including increased confidence, identifying solutions to problems, improved self-image, and increased self-esteem. Once this skill is mastered, it creates the perception that any challenge or situation that develops, is already something that has been confronted. By visualizing the challenges that confront any goal, you can figure out how to overcome them. This creates a sense that you

---

THE THREE STEPS

have already overcome those obstacles and have the necessary skills to do it again. If you can see it, you can achieve it!

When you visualize your target regularly, with strong emotion, you will see your goals "turn up" in your life-often by unexplainable coincidences, or simply by gradual improvements. The better you get at visualizing, the faster you'll start creating the life you want.

> *Visualization is a mental rehearsal. You create images in your mind doing whatever it is you want. When you get settled in a chair, close your eyes and allow yourself to see the situation. Then use your imagination to see yourself being successful, closing the deal, having the relationship, winning the game—whatever the goal is that you wish to achieve. Watch your success play itself out step, by step, over and over again. The key to visualizing is being present. Whatever you create with your "mind's eye" is real.*

Thumbs UP!

There is a common misconception about multi-tasking. There is strong belief that a person can do several actions at one time. Talking and texting while drive is considered the norm. Our society promotes and encourages the ability to take on

THE THREE STEPS

numerous responsibilities and tasks all at once.
However, it is scientifically impossible to focus on
more than one thing at one time. Here's the proof:

*Sit in a comfortable chair putting both feet
on the ground. Place both arms at your
side. Then, lift your right arm/hand upward
holding in front of you. Make a fist and put
your thumb in the upright position, giving the
"thumbs up" sign. Closing one eye, and
keeping the other eye open, focus directly
on your thumb for 30 seconds. Then take
your focus off of your thumb and focus on
something beyond your thumb, something
that may be on a distant wall for 30
seconds. Then focus on your thumb for 30
seconds. Then focus on the distant wall for
30 seconds. Now focus on both (your thumb
and the distant wall). What happens?*

It is not biologically possible to focus on two things
at one time. Your brain is not able to calculate more
than one image, concept, or thought at a time.
When it comes to goals, it is no different. It is
extremely important to stay focused on what you
really want. If you take your focus off the goal, it is
very likely you will have a much more difficult time
achieving it. There are numerous distractions that
will take your attention off of what you really want.
Stay focused on your goal.

THE THREE STEPS

Focus Thoughts

"Focus Thoughts" allow your mind to work in your favor. They are positive, resonate deep within you, and help you understand the possibilities. When an obstacle arises there is a built in mechanism to offset negative thinking. For your "Focus Thoughts" to be effective, use the following guidelines:

Make the thought genuine. Make the thought short. Make the thought truthful. Make the thought positive.

Focus Thought Examples:

> *By giving my best effort I can accomplish "X*
> *Using my best attitude I can do "X"*
> *The only thing that matters is "X"*

My Focus Thoughts:
I can do _____ because I am _____
Since other _____ have done _____, so can I
When I close my eyes I see _____

TEN LIFE PRINCIPLES

"OPPORTUNITYISNOWHERE"

Words have the power to transform life in an instant. They have the potential to unite a country, while simultaneously tearing down a culture. Words can be used to inspire, motivate and empower or to hurt, alienate, and demean. Some individuals have the incredible gift by sharing their words to move, engage and encourage people. Others can use their words while standing on stage to connect, dominate and influence. Take the word above. For some, it reads "opportunity is nowhere," for others it says, "opportunity is now here." It's all a matter of perspective and whether or not your eyes and mind focused on the word "no" or the word "now." Either way you read it, you are correct. However, ultimately it is up to you to make the interpretation as to what you take from that quote.

I am Somebody!

"I am somebody...I AM SOMEBODY." The motivational speaker stood at the front of the crowd screaming, "I am somebody!" As I heard him shout, it was clear he wanted us all to join, and so I did..."I am somebody, I am somebody...I AM SOMEBODY!" I wasn't sure why I jumped in, but everyone else was so it just seemed natural to do so.

45

TEN LIFE PRINCIPLES

It was a cold fall day and the sky was gray. It had a feeling of rain, and my biggest concern was hoping that I would not get wet if the clouds decided to open up. It was 1979, I was in the seventh grade and standing next to my classmates in a large High School football stadium. I had no idea who this person was, but it seemed that we were in the presence of "greatness." Or, at least that was what my teachers said. They kept saying how lucky and fortunate we were to be hearing the great Jessie Jackson. At first I did get very excited that my school would bring one of the greatest New York Yankees to come to visit and give us a pep talk. My friends and I were indeed going to see greatness and hear about Mr. October and his incredible baseball career. Because I heard the teacher say, "Reggie Jackson."

As the person stood cheering into the microphone, thrusting his right arm into the air repeatedly, the voice was not very familiar. In fact, as I looked closer at him it was obvious that this person was not Reggie Jackson. I became confused and leaned over to my teacher and said, "I thought you said that Reggie Jackson was going to speak," and in the type of look and

TEN LIFE PRINCIPLES

comment only a teacher can provide, she chuckled and said, "no, it's the Reverend Jessie Jackson." I said, "Jessie who?" Screaming she said, "Jessie Jackson the preacher. Now go on and join him...I am somebody, I am somebody, I am somebody."

The Blueprint of Life

Years ago I read an inspiring book by T. Harv Eker[8],*"Secrets of the Millionaire Mind"* (2005) It was a New York Times, Wall Street Journal, and USA Today Bestseller and it seemed like everyone I knew was reading it, referring to it, and demanding that it was changing their lives. From what I was hearing from my friends, colleagues and peers, Eker was able to articulate wealth and manifest certain financial circumstances in such a way, that it was in my best interest to read the book. He was offering workshops throughout the country and I was encouraged to attend, but reading the book was where I wanted to begin.

The book really was remarkable and when asked about books to read, it is one of the top ten books I recommend. Eker does an incredible job with his approach and has the ability to help the reader become more aware of their relationship with money and how to go about manifesting wealth in an empowering way. However, what I took from

TEN LIFE PRINCIPLES

that book had less to do about money, and more about how people learn and develop their relationship around money. He introduces the "Financial Blueprint" people have and his ability to identify their "blueprint" within a short amount of time simply by talking with them and asking a few short questions. The idea of a "blueprint" resonated within me and helped me realize that not only is Eker right in terms of a person's "Financial Blueprint," but also that most of us grow up with an overall "Life Blueprint."

In addition to Eker's book I also read *"The Four Agreements,"* (1997) by Don Miguel Ruiz[9]. As I read the first chapter, his writing about "domestication" connected deeply within me. I had not considered the idea of being domesticated to any extent and immediately had one of those "ah-ha" moments regarding my life. We do indeed domesticate our children and ourselves. Although the word domesticate has a strong connotation, I find it rather fitting when I speak with groups of people.

Upon completing these two books, I started thinking about my own life, the messages and lessons that I learned and believe in and realized that through my own life's experiences I was partial to an unexpected realization. The "Life Blueprint" we use is unknowingly forced upon us. It generally begins

TEN LIFE PRINCIPLES

to take root at the end of elementary school and the beginning of middle school. We quickly and easily buy into it, because it's so subtle and the message is given to us in the most vulnerable times in our lives -- adolescence. It begins with our parents, continues with our teachers', and policy and decision makers ensure it is repeated in the statistics. This "Life Blueprint" is repeated constantly in a number of various forms and it very rarely varies.

Once it is shared it will quickly resonate with you. It would not be at all surprising if you are able to immediately identify the times in your own life you bought into this "Blueprint." It is very likely this "Blueprint" has already become imbedded into your own life.

Life Blueprint

1. You have to study **HARD**
2. In order to get good **GRADES**
3. To get into a good **COLLEGE**
4. In order to get a good **JOB**
5. In order to make a lot of **MONEY**
6. And thereby becoming **HAPPY/ SUCCESSFUL**

Throughout the past several years as a trained professional coach, motivational speaker, and author, it has become more and more clear how

TEN LIFE PRINCIPLES

powerful this "blueprint" has become within our culture. Unfortunately though, each step in this "Blueprint" eventually creates the exact opposite of its intended purpose. Its like going to a physician, being diagnosed with a problem, then having the medical treatment create more health issues, rather than curing the original illness.

The Ten Life Principles are provided as an alternative "Blueprint" or a supplement of your current "Blueprint." They are meant to foster a clearer image and perspective in life. They are to be used in place of or in addition to your current coping skills, or thoughts. They have been tested, grappled with, and challenged. They have endured throughout the years, and in some cases over centuries.

All of these principles are based on learning, training, and implementation in my own personal and professional life. Please do not simply "believe" any of these principles at face value. They have been introduced to me at various times in my life and prove to provide the necessary guidance and support needed to understand and confront life's peaks and valleys. Furthermore, they coexist within the Law of Attraction helping establish a more positive mindset.

TEN LIFE PRINCIPLES

Mindset

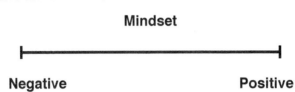

Negative   **Positive**

Carol S. Dweck[10], in her book "Mindset: The New Psychology of Success" (2006) offers a remarkable approach to understanding a person's mindset. Although there is no mention of the Law of Attraction, her exceptional psychological understanding of the mind offers an alternative approach to behavior and challenges. She identifies the two types of mindset as fixed and growth. A person with a fixed mindset often sticks to what they know and how to handle challenges. A person with a growth mindset is open to alternative ideas and approaches. However, in terms of LOA it is best to use the term positive and negative mindset.

Take a moment and think about someone you know who is negative. What are the characteristics and qualities? How do you feel when you think about this person? Now think about someone you know who is positive. What are those characteristics and qualities? How do you feel when you think about that person? People who are positive send out energy that is mutually contagious. Even when thinking about that person, they make you feel good on the inside. Likewise, a person who is

51

TEN LIFE PRINCIPLES

negative has the opposite effect. It is a simple concept that addresses an important strategy for success. As a professional coach, any person has the ability to adjust their mindset. Take the different colored glasses exercise and anyone can change their perspective. The Life Principles are additional tools that can be utilized to engage a positive mindset allowing individuals an empowering perspective. If given the choice, would you rather select a negative mindset, or positive?

LIFE PRINCIPLE ONE
I Am Who I Choose To Be

The uniqueness of this principle focuses on two things-choice and being. First, one of the major elements that separates humans from other animals on the planet is free will. We have the ability to choose nearly every aspect of our life. Everything in life is a choice. Even when you feel you are between a "rock and a hard place" you have choice. How you live your life is no different.

Secondly, we are human beings, not human doings. Yet, nearly everyone focuses on all the things they are doing. "What do you do for a living?" is a common question when two strangers meet for the first time. We focus on the necessary actions that need to be accomplished to achieve various goals. Imagine if there really was a choice in "being." Our choices impact what we all do, but it is

TEN LIFE PRINCIPLES

essential to focus on being. Being is a state of mind, something that can be controlled by attitude and thought. Doing is based on action which is impacted by those thoughts and attitude. Success, satisfaction, and happiness are not actions, they are components of free will and a state of being.

You have the power to choose the life you want to lead. You have the power to choose your thoughts and dreams. Jim Valvano was facing terminal cancer and how he chose to live out his life was memorialized in his speech in 1993.

"Don't Give Up...Don't Ever Give Up"
Jim Valvano, Arthur Ashe Award
1993 ESPYs[11]

"When people say to me how do you get through life or each day, it's the same thing. To me, there are three things we all should do every day. We should do this every day of our lives. Number one is laugh. You should laugh every day. Number two is think. You should spend some time in thought. Number three is you should have your emotions moved to tears, could be happiness or joy. But think about it. If you laugh, you think and you cry, that's a full day. That's a heck of a day. You do that seven days a week, you're going to have something special...

TEN LIFE PRINCIPLES

…That's what I'm going to try to do every minute that I have left. I will thank God for the day and the moment I have. If you see me, smile and give me a hug. That's important to me too. But try if you can to support, whether it's AIDS or the cancer foundation, so that someone else might survive, might prosper and might actually be cured of this dreaded disease. I can't thank ESPN enough for allowing this to happen. I'm going to work as hard as I can for cancer research and hopefully, maybe, we'll have some cures and some breakthroughs. I'd like to think, I'm going to fight my brains out to be back here again next year for the Arthur Ashe recipient. I want to give it next year!"

LIFE PRINCIPLE TWO
There Are No Mistakes, Only Opportunities

When does a mistake become a mistake? How many times did you wake up in the morning and say to yourself, "I'm going to make a mistake today!" How come mistakes are mostly perceived as something bad?

Numerous times I have watched individuals on tv following some type of significant scandal where they apologize to their loved ones and constituents by saying, "I'm sorry, I made a mistake." By saying

TEN LIFE PRINCIPLES

that, it somehow absolves them of responsibility and allows them to be accepted as being "human."

When Michael Vick faced the media in August 2007, he stood on the podium and said, "I'm sorry for making a mistake..." and then proceeded to share the number of mistakes he had made. It was honest and sincere, but he was still going to be imprisoned for supporting illegal dog fitting. What immediately came to mind, was the length of time he was involved with the illegal operation. From what was gathered, he spent at least five years, paying for, supporting, and warehousing this operation. How many days during that five year period did he wake up and say, "I"m making a mistake today." My guess is probably not once! So, when did it become a mistake? When he got caught. If he doesn't get caught, there is no mistake. What he really did was make a choice, over and over and over again. Until, someone caught him and held him accountable. The so called mistake was judgement based on hindsight. Mistakes only occur after the fact. The question then becomes, what did Michael Vick learn from that choice?

Think about the number of mistakes made in your life? How many are there? If you were facing the exact situations once again, without having the knowledge of what you learned from those

TEN LIFE PRINCIPLES

experiences, you would make the same exact decision that you made then. Thereby, life is full of choices and decisions, the concept of a mistake is only an interpretation labeled by someone over a decision that did not end up with the intended outcome. It then becomes a learning opportunity on how not to make a similar choice in the future.

The decisions you make stem from your mind and heart. You make choices based on your past, your belief system and your collective life experience. Once this principle is integrated into your life, you will no longer beat yourself up over "mistakes," but rather ask yourself, "what is the lesson and what can be learned from this experience?"

Formula 409®

Formula 409® is an all-purpose antibacterial cleaner owned by Clorox® that cleans, disinfects and deodorizes. It was first invented in 1957 by Morris D. Rouff that manufactured industrial strength cleaners. In 1960 it was sold to Chemsol for a low six-figure amount and eventually to Clorox in the late 1970s for $7 million.

One of the biggest urban legends surrounding this product is how it was named. Some said it was the birthdate of the inventor's wife, while others stated it

TEN LIFE PRINCIPLES

was the area code for which the inventors lived. However, the Formula 409® name is actually a tribute to the tenacity of two young Detroit scientists determined on formulating the greatest grease-cutting, dirt-destroying, bacteria cutting cleaner on the planet.

Thing is, creating the ultimate cleaner didn't just happen on the first try. And it didn't happen on the 101st or the 301st either. It wasn't until batch number 409 that they were finally satisfied. And so, the name stuck. Formula 409®. That means, the scientists made a mistake 408 times, before they finally got it right. Or rather, they learned 408 times how not to make the greatest industrial cleaner ever invented. Then on the 409th, they got it right!

LIFE PRINCIPLE THREE
I Am A Product Of My Belief System

Most people do not take the time to consider their belief system, how it gets created, how it is influenced and how it impacts choices made in life. In general, when individuals hear "belief system" it is mostly interpreted as religious. Although that is often the case, in this situation a person's belief system is only partly impacted by their religion, with other outside factors playing a much larger role. No

3

TEN LIFE PRINCIPLES

two people look at the world in the same way. Everyone has a 'belief filter' that impacts life experiences. However, as Napoleon Bonaparte once said, "History is a myth that men agree to believe."

The creation of your belief system began the day you were born, and so did your myth. If you are male, you received blue items. If you are female, you received pink. As you got older, boys were focused more on cars, sports and predominately male dominated areas. While girls were focused more on dance, theater and female-related areas.

A fun activity to test your personal beliefs is to create a diagram of the home where you grew up. Design the rooms as best as you can remember, while allowing yourself to "feel" the memories that were created in each room. Then, once completed, go back and identify the messages and values that were directly, and indirectly provided to you. Think about what you learned about love, happiness, success, money, risks, failure, careers, family, etc. Whether you realized it at the moment or not, your home created a significant foundation for your belief system. The same exercise can be used for any other location where you either lived, or worked for a lengthy period of time. Do this with your grandparents home, or your first job, or a sports team that was relevant.

3

CHAPTER THREE

TEN LIFE PRINCIPLES

Beliefs are only effective when they help promote the person you want to be. You do not need to continue using the beliefs that inhibit success any longer. Your beliefs are also a personal myth and only a reality because you choose to see them that way. You can chose to no longer rely on beliefs that have become irrelevant or worthless in the present.

One of the most popular stories shared with children about the American Revolution highlights the amazing journey of Paul Revere. This story is told over and over with an eventual understanding over the truth bound in these experiences.

The Legend of Paul Revere

Poets, historians, and schoolbooks have retold the legendary ride of Paul Revere for more than two centuries. The most influential is the epic poem by Henry Wadsworth Longfellow where Paul Revere is credited as the sole rider who alerted the colonies that the British were coming.

> Listen my children and you shall hear
> Of the midnight ride of Paul Revere,
> On the eighteenth of April, in Seventy-five;
> Hardly a man is now alive
> Who remembers that famous day and year?

Thanks to Longfellow, there is no scholar or school child alive that does not know the

59

TEN LIFE PRINCIPLES

name of Paul Revere, and why he was important. However, most people do not know that Longfellow took some liberties by embellishing the story.

Paul Revere was born in Boston in 1734 to a French father and Bostonian mother. He started his young life training to be a silversmith. After the death of his father in 1754, he enlisted in the provincial army to fight in the French and Indian War. As his life progressed he became more and more frustrated with his own financial difficulties and joined the Sons of Liberty, a group of men initially responsible for organizing early revolution efforts.

On the night of April 18, 1775, Revere was sent to signal Charlestown that the British troops were on the move. "The British are coming" is often the phrase mostly associated with this legend. However, contrary to popular beliefs, he never said anything remotely like that. In addition, Revere was not the only one riding throughout the towns. Revere actually only spent a short period of time riding approximately 19 miles. The truth of the matter was that there were a total of four men and one woman that made those late

TEN LIFE PRINCIPLES

night rides, alerting the early Americans of what dangers lay ahead. They were Paul Revere, Samuel Prescott, Israel Bissell, William Dawes, and Sybil Ludington.

Israel Bissell was the rider that actually spent the most amount of time riding in and out of towns, traveling for four days and six hours covering nearly 350 miles. He rode from Watertown, MA through Philadelphia, and ended up in Hartford, CT. It was Bissell that deserved to be the legend, not Revere. The American poet and historian, Clay Perry, in the manner of Longfellow, wrote an ode to Bissell with these opening lines:

Listen, my children, to my epistle
Of the long, long ride of Israel Bissell,
Who outrode Paul by miles and time
But didn't rate a poet's rhyme.

But, Longfellow's poem sounds much better so the Legend of Paul Revere lives on.

LIFE PRINCIPLE FOUR
A Purpose Can Be Found In
Everything That Happens

When people have negative outcomes in life, they say, "Well it's okay, things happen for a reason." It's an attempt to place a pseudo-positive spin on the situation. However, it really does not provide any

TEN LIFE PRINCIPLES

true solution. It can leave someone unfulfilled because the reason is unknown? Think about it- someone says, "Things happen for a reason." You respond, "What's the reason?" Their response back would be, "I don't know. But, things do happen for a reason."

The statement is supposed to provide hope, but it is that reason that seems out of our control. That may be acceptable to some, however a more positive approach can be finding a purpose in what happens. It provides a personal insight and direction to control what the "purpose" may be. Accepting what happens, both good and bad, then creating the meaning on why it occurred allows for learning, growth and greater control.

Purpose is similar to meaning. Purpose allows a person to place meaning to the particular outcome. It allows the person to become directly involved with the outcome. Some people are more prone to find meaning than others. Some individuals may believe in fate and believe life is predestined. Therefore, they are more comfortable with the idea that things happen for a reason. Others may believe there are hidden messages and signs embedded in their own life events. Sort of like a puzzle or game to be discovered and explored. The purpose may not be immediately clear, but discovering it is empowering.

TEN LIFE PRINCIPLES

Everything does or doesn't happen for a reason, it's really up to you.

The Loss of Loved Ones

My mom died on April 11, 2002, following a week-long fight against sepsis and strep pneumonia. The week before we were together in Los Angeles on a family vacation. As we hugged and said good-bye it was obvious she was not feeling well. I encouraged her husband to take her to the hospital immediately. However, they had a long ride home to Arizona and he promised to take her the following morning if she was not any better. Tragically, overnight, she collapsed on her way to the bathroom. An ambulance rushed her to the hospital where doctors quickly diagnosed renal (kidney) failure. She was intubated, placed in the ICU, and connected to life-support machines. She laid motionless surviving by tubes, science, medical interventions, and prayers. Over the course of the next few days her prognosis was a roller coaster of peaks and valleys. The constant change of uncertainty took me on an uncharted ride of emotions. Eventually, the pulmonologist pulled us aside to share the stark reality. We were faced with a no-win decision. Was she

TEN LIFE PRINCIPLES

really "living" or was it the medical
technology keeping her alive?

We huddled outside her room stunned by
the untenable situation. I was furious, sad,
scared and confused. How fair was it for a
child to make a decision such as this for a
parent? Only a few days before we were
eating dinner together. The choice to stop
the machines was not easy, but after a hard
discussion, reality superseded the
conversation.

As the nurses slowly prepared my mom for
the machines to be turned off, we stood
around her hoping for a last minute miracle.
One by one, a button was pushed, a wire as
disconnected, until eventually there was no
sound in the room. The silence was
deafening. I started to scream, "Breathe
mom, breathe" over and over again. I
wanted one more chance to tell her I loved
her. One more chance to say thank you for
being my parent. One more chance to say
good-bye.

What seemed like eternity was less than a
minute. We watched her face turn a shade
of purple and blue, highlighting her difficulty
filling her lungs with the needed oxygen.
Then, the struggle stopped, the skin color

64

TEN LIFE PRINCIPLES

returned to normal, and she laid there, dead and in peace.

The phone call that came at 10 o'clock on Sunday morning, March 20, 2005, changed my life forever. When I answered it was my brother's father-in-law on the end of the line. He didn't mince words. He said that Mark (my younger brother) was dead. Not much else comes to mind with the remainder of the call. But, my best guess was they really weren't sure why and how it happened. Something occurred overnight. My brother's snoring was so loud, my sister-in-law ended up going into another room to sleep. A choice that she had never done before and probably lives to regret to this day. But the reality was that he was no longer alive. It was the most unsettling calls I have ever received. When I hung up, I sat in silence as my wife wanted to know what was going on. Then a flood of emotions and questions came to mind. As I looked at my wife in incredible pain and confusion I realized there were no answers. Just the certainty that Mark was no longer alive. I was puzzled, shocked and in extreme pain.

Over the years, actually decades, my brother and mother fought, argued and

TEN LIFE PRINCIPLES

often chose not to speak to one another. Silence was a "golden" tool that was a learned strategy when family was mad with one another. Instead of dealing with the conflict directly, silence was used allowing feelings and thoughts to fester and grow. I watched my younger brother grow up and live a life hating our mother. I watched my mother go from being loving and kind, to being spiteful, hurtful and resentful.

At the time my mother died, I had just persuaded Mark to consider reuniting with our mom. He was reluctant, but decided to give it a try. The week prior to her death, we were all together in Los Angeles where my brother lived with his wife and kids. It was actually a positive experience and was the next step to rebuilding their relationship. However, that week was the last time we ever spent together.

The fall out from her passing was disastrous. It turned out that my mother, by the encouragement of her husband, wrote my brother out of her will. Needless to say, that action was extremely painful for my brother opening old wounds that would last until the day he died.

TEN LIFE PRINCIPLES

The day of my brother's funeral I noticed he was being buried only a few feet from my mother's site. Throughout the ceremony and for many days that followed the placement of his final resting place troubled me. The irony of them being buried so closed disturbed me deeply. How could two people who hated each other so openly on Earth be placed so close to one another for eternity?

During the initial mourning phase (shiva), I asked numerous family members and friends their rationale for that situation. Most simply said, "Things happen for a reason." However, all that comment did was make me feel further confused, even angry. As if there was a reason, but I wasn't privy to it. Then I spent time with a Rabbi.

This Rabbi had been a dear friend for a number of years and a spiritual leader in my life. I had tremendous respect and appreciation for him. I asked him the same question that was troubling me for days. How come my mother and brother were buried so close together for eternity, when they were so hateful and angry towards one another while living? His answer transformed my thinking instantaneously.

TEN LIFE PRINCIPLES

He explained "each person has a soul and their body is a vessel in which it lives." Throughout life, this vessel "moves from place to place protecting the soul. Then, when life expires, the soul moves onto heaven and the vessel remains here on Earth." The vessel contains all of the negative that occurs in life, while the soul goes on with love. He continued, by saying when my mother gave "birth to my brother, her love was unconditional and her soul and my brother's soul were one." It was only "after time here on Earth that the bad outweighed the good." When she died, "Her vessel was left behind, while her soul went to heaven." She passed away first in order for her to accept Mark when it was his turn to die. "Just like she was there unconditionally the day he was born, she was there to be with him the day he died. Leaving behind his vessel on Earth and his soul was reconnected to hers."

In that explanation, I found the purpose of her death, my brother's death and the location of their burial sites. It made sense and I have been accepting of those losses since that time.

TEN LIFE PRINCIPLES

LIFE PRINCIPLE FIVE
The Only Constant Is Change

Everything is in constant motion and continual change. Atoms are in constant motion in all physical objects, no matter how solid and stationary they may seem. It is easy to notice that the bodies of all living creatures are constantly changing, not only aging but also going through various biological processes and exchanges with the environment. Hair grows out, finger nails get longer, babies grow into children then into adolescents, that eventually become adults. Skin starts to wrinkle, eyesight goes bad, hearing becomes a challenge, the heart gets clogged with cholesterol.

Everyone is dealing with change in one way or another. Living in change is a natural occurrence allowing us to grow, develop and flourish. Many people equate change with some type of negative outcome. However, change is really part of an evolution, not revolution. True, there are times that require drastic change in a particular moment, but a life cannot grow without constant change.

Once change is accepted as a regular component in life we can release the desire to control and acknowledge that change is part of life. We all have the choice to adapt to the change and develop skills to cope with it. Without change we cease to exist as a society.

TEN LIFE PRINCIPLES

Heraclitus of Ephesus

Heraclitus was an ancient Greek philosopher who lived about 100 years before Plato. Historians claim he was the first philosopher that understood the significance of change and how society is in a constant state of flux. He believed that change was inevitable not something to be controlled.

Eventually referred to as "the Dark One," Heraclitus was well aware of change and how nothing is ever the same. He was the first to acknowledge that nothing in the physical world ever stays the same. Everything needs to move or change if it's going to progress and grow.

The saying that sparked the biggest debate was, "You cannot step into the same river twice." If you put a foot into a river, by the time you take it out, the water has flooded over it thereby creating change in the water. If you put your foot in again, the river is no longer the same river you put your foot into originally. The constant movement of the water creates a continual change in the river-no two currents are the same, no two places in the water are the same. Whether Heraclitus was purposeful in his insight, or

TEN LIFE PRINCIPLES

simply judging a situational outcome, people have come to understand that one must accept that change is a constant and necessary part of life.

LIFE PRINCIPLE SIX
Pain Is Inevitable, Suffering Is Optional

There is a saying among parents regarding their own happiness, "I am only as happy as my saddest child." Any parent who has watched their child deal with pain, emotional or physical, understands how challenging it can be. I have yet to meet any parent that wants their child to experience any type of discomfort. Pain hurts, it creates feelings that can be unexplainable, while putting certain life choices in motion in hopes of avoiding further discomfort.

Even though people have different thresholds for pain, it is nearly impossible to *not* experience some type of pain in life. Pain is everywhere, in everything, in nearly every moment. What is painful to one person, may not be painful to someone else. One person may experience pain and withdraw, another person may experience an identical pain and persevere. Pain is inevitable.

There are a few people in the world that cannot feel pain. It is a rare genetic disorder known as CIPA (Congenital Insensitivity to Pain with Anhidrosis). Individuals with this illness are literally unable to

TEN LIFE PRINCIPLES

feel pain. It may seem to be a "blessing" to not feel pain, yet for parents this is actually a "curse."

Imagine your child being inflicted by this disease. A bowl of scalding hot soup is placed in front of your child. He/She immediately grabs a spoon taking some out of the bowl and placing it in his/her mouth. They will not be able to feel the pain associated with the hot liquid. It will immediately burn their tongue, cheek and throat. Or a fresh batch of chocolate chip cookies have just come out of the oven. You place them safely on top of the counter, then the phone rings. You go an answer it and turn your back momentarily to the hot rack of cookies. Your child comes into the kitchen, the aroma of fresh baked cookies in the air and grabs some to eat. The child will not feel the pain from the heat that creates blisters on his/her hand, nor be able to feel the discomfort and burning of her tongue, mouth and esophagus.

Pain exists for a reason. It is actually a great educator, maybe the best. Through pain we learn what experiences we do not want to repeat, or what it takes to get to what we really want. Throughout life we all encounter peaks and valleys, illness, sickness and pain. Some seem worse than others, but once we face some physical and/or emotional horrors we often look at our situation and question the circumstances. To truly appreciate happiness,

TEN LIFE PRINCIPLES

one must experience what it feels like to be unhappy. To experience pain, one must face joy. However, its up to the individual to acknowledge the situation and then choose how to deal with it; suffering is a choice. There is no rainbow without the storm.

The Butterfly

When a caterpillar is born it spends the first weeks of its life eating voraciously. It doubles, then triples in size. In a short time, it finds a resting place and begins a tremendous transformation. It creates a chrysalis when it transitions itself from a caterpillar into a butterfly. When the creature is ready, it begins to make its way out of the chrysalis and into the world.

One day, a boy spent hours watching a butterfly struggle to emerge from its chrysalis. It managed to make a small hole, but its body was too large to get through it. After a long battle, it appeared to be exhausted and remained absolutely still.

The boy wanted to help the butterfly and went to get a pair of scissors to open the chrysalis. As he went searching for the scissors his mother asked what he was doing. He told his mom the story and how

73

TEN LIFE PRINCIPLES

he wanted to open the chrysalis, thus helping the butterfly.

The mom immediately stopped him and asked him how that was going to help the butterfly. The boy explained that by opening the cocoon it would make it easier for the butterfly to be freed. The mom smiled at the boys kindness but explained that by doing that it would actually have an opposite effect. Confused, the boy asked why.

The mother explained that in the chrysalis, a butterfly's body is very small, wrinkled and its wings are weak. Even though his act seems to be helpful allowing the butterfly to open its wings and fly away it would, in fact, ultimately harm the butterfly. It would spend the rest of its brief life dragging around its shrunken body and shriveled wings, incapable of flight. It would die within minutes.

What the boy—out of kindness and his eagerness to help—had failed to understand was that the tightness of the chrysalis and the efforts that the butterfly has to make to squeeze out of that tiny hole were nature's way of training the butterfly and of strengthening its wings. The "pain" the butterfly was experiencing was essential to

TEN LIFE PRINCIPLES

its overall survival. The boy interpreted the pain incorrectly, wanting to stop what was being witnessed.

LIFE PRINCIPLE SEVEN
Life Is A Perceptual Illusion

Life is a television show. Life is a game. Life is a movie. Life is social media. Life is all of those things and more. If life is a game, then who's your coach?

Perception is the lens that is used to interpret a situation, circumstance or outcome.

Illusion is an image that is either designed to deceive or mislead reality, or it convinces us that the real life version of an object is untrue or false.

Depending where you live, who your parents are, what language you speak, the religion (or not) you are raised with, the ancestry of your family, the culture that surrounds you, where you go (went) to school...there are so many factors that form your life, perception and the illusion you have. There is no "right way" to live life, yet the lessons that are learned very early on seem to dictate a formalized process that determines what your experience here on Earth is supposed to be. Consider the "Life Blueprint" mentioned previously. The focus of success and happiness is so vital to so many people, yet ultimately the definition and

TEN LIFE PRINCIPLES

understanding of achieving that goal is really just a conditional illusion taught over and over again by family, friends, teachers, etc.

Research has proven that the world and your life is a creation of your perceptions. Whether it's the focus of money, the relevance of giving charity, or deciding to stop a cultural tradition, whatever we focus on and expect to see is what we attract in our life. If you do not like what you see, you can create a different and more meaningful perception. Understanding that your perceptions create a prism, at any moment you can develop something entirely new.

~The Soul of Money (2003)~
Lynne Twist[12]

In America, money often becomes the focus for each individual. Not just having a little bit, but having a lot of it. Given the blueprint for success, money is the epitome of achievement. In our capitalistic environment, money seems to be the driving factor that determines whether or not a person is able to achieve greatness. Money dictates who you are, where you are headed and the ability to get there. Money is not the only thing, it's everything. Money is power.

TEN LIFE PRINCIPLES

Twist identifies the element of scarcity that often interrupts our sense of inadequacy in life. Scarcity is not real, but it is passed down as a truth that remains a focal point of disappointment. We believe that there is "not enough," "the more we have the better," and that there "is nothing that can be done" with our current situation. Life is what it is.

Each person defines him/herself based on the amount of money in their pocket. The power of money is derived from the power we give to it. Money is about allocation, over accumulation, or whatever we do with it rather than how much we keep.

Twist was speaking in the late 1970s, in Harlem to an audience who were living in poverty. She was speaking about the Hunger Project and was fundraising for the cause at the time. She was in a basement of an old church filled with the plink-plink of drips from leaking ceilings hitting buckets below. After talking about the Project's commitment in Africa, it came time to request donations.

After dead silence, Gertrude, a gray-haired woman stood up. "Now, I ain't got no checkbook and I ain't go no credit cards. To me, money is a lot like water. For some

TEN LIFE PRINCIPLES

folks it rushes through their life like a raging river. Money comes through my life like a little trickle. But I want to pass it on in a way that does the most good for the most folks. I see that as my right and as my responsibility. It is also my joy. I have fifty dollars in my purse that I earned from doing a white woman's wash and I want to give it to you." Money meant something else to Gertrude.

LIFE PRINCIPLE EIGHT
I Am Greater Than I Appear To Be

A tremendous amount of money, energy and time is spent on appearance. The clothing and textile business is nearly a $3 trillion industry. In 2010 the US Census Bureau stated that a household income of $50,000 per year spent roughly $2,000 per year, on clothing. How you look and whether or not one is skinny, blond, short, tall, male, or female has a significant impact on the way our media portrays those who can become successful.

Like it or not, you are being judged on how you look, what you wear, where you go, and how you carry yourself. The news we see, the movies we watch, the stories that impact us the most all focus on how we look, convey ourselves, and measure our physical features. Appearance becomes a primary emphasis in middle school, reaches a peak

TEN LIFE PRINCIPLES

of importance in high school, and then shifts to varying degrees in career and job searches in college and thereafter. Research has proven that tall people get paid more money, over weight people get paid less, blondes get paid more, workers who workout get paid more, and women who wear makeup make more. It seems that nearly every where within our society we are mainly critiqued by our appearance, from a child going to school to an adult getting a job.

The vulnerabilities created by the obsession with outward appearance causes numerous troubles. To overcome these difficult hazards of mental growth, emotional maturity, and social intelligence a person must be able to look within him/herself. Those that preserve a strong core value system can utilize those to protect their external actions. A current craze impacting Millennials is something called, FOMO - Fear Of Missing Out. Given the immediacy, social media, connect now behavior with smart phones, it is extremely easy to feel left out of perceived important activities. Whether it is not being a part of a group picture on Facebook, seeing close friends post a something on Instagram that does not include you, or not being included in a SnapChat story, one can easily succumb to the psychological impacts of not being a part of others events. An individual with strong principles and an

---

TEN LIFE PRINCIPLES

unwavering sense of character is able to overcome the pressure created by FOMO.

Ralph Waldo Emerson once said, "What lies behind us and what lies before us are small matters compared to what lies within us. And when we bring what is within us out into the world, miracles happen." You are a powerful, resourceful and incredibly gifted individual. You have a unique gift to share regardless of how you see yourself. You are truly greater than you can possibly imagine. Once you open yourself up to this principle you will reach your dreams and all of your aspirations, because you are simply amazing.

Internal Greatness

In 1995, a computer programmer, *Pierre Omidyar* started auctioning off items from his personal website. When the amount of web traffic made it necessary to upgrade to a business Internet account, he started charging fees. The site is now known as *eBay*.

After operating convenience stores in southern California, *Joe Coulombe* had an idea that college grads might want something better than 7-11. So he opened a tropical-themed market in Pasadena, stocked it with good wine and alcohol, hired

TEN LIFE PRINCIPLES

good people, and paid them well. He added more locations near universities, then healthy foods, and that's how *Trader Joe's* got started.

Phil Robertson loved duck hunting so much he chose that over playing professional football for the NFL. He invented a duck call, started a company called Duck Commander spawning a media and merchandising empire for a family known as *Duck Dynasty*.

In 1917, a young Japanese 23-year-old apprentice, *Konosuke Matsushita* with no formal education came up with an improved light socket. His boss wasn't interested so he started making samples in his basement. He later expanded with battery-powered bicycle lamps and other electronic products. Matsushita Electric, as it was known until 2008 when the company officially changed its name to *Panasonic*, is now worth $66 billion.

During the 1970s, J*ohn Ferolito and Don Vultaggio*, a couple of Brooklyn friends started a beer distributor out of the back of an old VW bus. Two decades later they decided to try their hand at soft drinks and launched *AriZona Green Tea*. Today,

---

TEN LIFE PRINCIPLES

AriZona teas are #1 in America and distributed worldwide.

LIFE PRINCIPLE NINE
Life Is A Journey, Not A Destination

Most individuals feel a tremendous release of stress when they hear this principle for the first time, in particular high school students. In their state of mind, they often believe the destination in life is college. It is a place that is referred to frequently beginning in middle school, and picks up steam as they enter their Freshman year. By their Junior year, the only focus is preparing for the national exams that will further determine whether or not they will get into college. Not just any college, but a good college.

Upon graduation from college an amazing realization occurs. They recognize that college was not the ultimate "destination." After a while, life is nothing more than a number of destinations. They are landmark moments connected by various life experiences.

A Headstone

When was the last time you visited a cemetery? Next time you go, look closely at the headstones. Notice what is etched in the stones. Names, date of birth, date of death, various titles like father, mother,

TEN LIFE PRINCIPLES

son, daughter can be seen on each one. Depending on religion you will see various symbols highlighting a personal belief, or some type of relevant saying. However, what is the most important part on the stone? What identifies the time they spent on Earth? The part of the headstone that reflects a person's journey is "the dash" between the dates. In her poem, "The Dash,"[13] Linda Ellis (1996) captures the significance of that little image. The dash signifies a person's life of how they lived-what they did or didn't do, and/or accomplish or didn't accomplish.

Life is a journey with peaks and valleys, high points and low points, moments of greatness sprinkled with elements of the mundane. Your life is an amazing journey with turns and spins, ups and downs at every given moment. It is a ride to be enjoyed and engaged. How will you live your dash?

New York Giants Super Bowl XLII Championship Season

During the 2007 NFL season, the New York Giants football team recorded an average 10 wins and 6 losses qualifying them as a wild card team for the playoffs. The odds of them winning the Super Bowl at the beginning of the season were 30 to 1. The New England Patriots, on the other hand,

TEN LIFE PRINCIPLES

made history that season by going
undefeated in the regular season winning all
sixteen games. The odds of winning the
championship were 5 to 1.

The road to Super Bowl XLII was not easy
for the Giants. Their first game, against the
Tampa Bay Buccaneers was their first
playoff victory since the 2000 NFC
Championship Game, and their first road
playoff game since the 1990 NFC
Championship Game. The final score was
24-14.

The following week, during the Divisional
Playoff game, they faced their nemesis the
Dallas Cowboys in Texas Stadium for the
third time that season. The Cowboys won
both previous games handedly. The game
seesawed back and forth up until the final
drive when Tony Romo's pass was
intercepted with :09 seconds left in the
game. The final score was 21-17 and
marked the first time in 20 years that the
NFC's #1 seeded team had been eliminated
in the divisional round.

Then they faced the Green Bay Packers in
the NFC Conference Championship game.
It was played in frigid conditions, with a
game time temperature of 0°F/-18°C and a

TEN LIFE PRINCIPLES

wind chill of −23°F/-30°C. The game was a
well-balanced battle ending with a score of
20-20 at the end of regulation requiring over
time (OT). Green Bay won the coin toss to
start the extra period. However, on the
second play of overtime a pass was
intercepted in Green Bay's territory setting
up a 47-yard field goal attempt to win the
game. The Giants, the NFC's #5 seed,
became just the second NFC wild card team
ever to win a conference championship and
the third team ever (and first NFC team) to
reach the Super Bowl with three playoff
wins on the road. The game is considered
one of the NFL's Greatest Games and often
referred to as "The Chilling Championship."

Meanwhile, the road to the Super Bowl for
the New England Patriots was a bit
different. Continuing their undefeated
season, they rolled through the playoffs
winning their two games at home. They
defeated the Jacksonville Jaguars and the
San Diego Chargers. New England veered
towards completing the unimaginable
undefeated season. They were a strong 18
wins and 0 losses entering Super Bowl XLII.

The Patriots entered the championship
game as a 12 point favorite after becoming

TEN LIFE PRINCIPLES

the first team to complete a perfect regular season since the 1972 Miami Dolphins. The Giants were seeking to become the first NFC wild card team to win a Super Bowl. The game was also a rematch of the final game of the regular season, in which New England won, 38–35.

The game is regarded as one of the biggest upsets in the history of sports. It is best remembered for the Giants' fourth-quarter game-winning drive as they were down 14–10 with 2:39 left in the game. New York got the ball on their own 17-yard line and marched 83 yards down the field to win the game.

In the locker room following the game, amongst the celebration, reporters were getting comments from the players about their unprecedented victory. The elation for accomplishing what seemed to be the impossible, was the notion of the journey it took for them to complete the ultimate task. From the end of the season to their victory in the Super Bowl, each play, each down represented an opportunity to become greater. One victory led to another, the more they played, the better they became, and the more they believed in their skills and

TEN LIFE PRINCIPLES

ability. Furthermore, the bonding that took place, and the strength of those relationships were far more valuable than any one of those games. Sure, they were football champions of the world, but the challenges and journey it took to put them there was far more valuable and meaningful.

LIFE PRINCIPLE TEN
Challenges Are Opportunities For Growth

One of the biggest fears people have, is the "fear of failure." They spend a bulk of their life doing whatever they can to avoid the pain and disappointment associated with failure. Very early on in life, children learn that failure is bad and there are unpleasant consequences if that occurs. Avoiding mistakes becomes the required focus to limit the pain in life.

Consider the Pain-Pleasure Principle[14] that was first introduced by Dr. Sigmund Freud in the early 1920s. Most people live life by making decisions and avoiding pain. They endure by doing whatever can be done to not be hurt by any choice. It's a principle that may not be a primary thought with individuals, but when faced with a difficult situation, the first thought that comes to mind is generally what can be done to ensure I do not feel any pain.

TEN LIFE PRINCIPLES

Academically we further exacerbate this fear by our institutionalized grading system. Which, by many standards is archaic and based in past glory. Apparently the earliest record of a letter-grade system comes from Mount Holyoke College in Massachusetts in 1897. They used a system that offered the letter grades of A, B, C, D or E. The Letter 'A' was excellent, 'B' was good, 'C' was fair, and 'D' was passing. At that time, E was the letter associated with failure. However, over the course of time, the letter E for failure was changed to the letter F. Guess why? There is not a teacher, or parent that has ever embraced a student who gets report cards with Fs. If an F is on a report card, the student is chastised, yelled at and debased for their effort.

What is interesting is the evolution of letter grades and the significance of why an E is not an option at most educational institutions. Since Fail starts with the letter F, what would an A equal? Not many words really capture what an A is, but how about the word Awesome. Then B would equal...Better than good? C would equal Chump and D, is easy, as that equals Dumb. Now, the problem with E. That's because E could actually mean Excellent. There cannot be an Excellent between Dumb and Fail, so the letter E is simply tossed out and ignored. E was replaced with F, because "F for failed" was more intuitive than "E for ... excellent or

TEN LIFE PRINCIPLES

failed?" That way, focus on failure could be much easier.

Speak with nearly any high school student. One of their biggest fears is failure and making a mistake. Student athletes are the same. They will do everything they can to avoid mistakes and failure in athletics. Some coaches will scream at them, berate them and humiliate them when failure occurs. We have created a generation of young adults who fear a life experience that is unavoidable. Life is full of mistakes, errors and failures. Life is full of obstacles.

More than 100 years ago, Friedrich Nietzsche wrote, "That which does not kill us outright makes us stronger." Challenges are constantly present throughout life. Research has proven that people who experience challenges earlier in their life are often happier than those that did not. Therefore, "helicopter" and "snow plow" parents actually end up doing more harm to their children then good. Protecting a child from difficulties is not only unreasonable, it is unhealthy. Individuals that embrace challenges end up being happier and more successful. Obstacles are not to be avoided, they are there for learning. The struggle that comes from challenges makes you a stronger (and happier) individual in the long run.

TEN LIFE PRINCIPLES

The Farmer and The Mule

An old mule fell into the farmer's well. The farmer heard the mule praying or whatever mules do when they fall into wells. After carefully assessing the situation, the farmer sympathized with the mule, but decided that neither the mule nor the well was worth the trouble of saving.

Instead, he called his neighbors together, told them what had happened, and enlisted them to help haul dirt to bury the old mule in the well and put him out of his misery.

Initially the old mule was hysterical! But as the farmer and his neighbors continued shoveling and the dirt hit his back, a thought struck him. It suddenly dawned on him that every time a load of dirt landed on his back, HE WOULD SHAKE IT OFF AND STEP UP! This he did, blow after blow. "Shake it off and step up...shake it off and step up... shake it off and step up!" He repeated to encourage himself. No matter how painful the blows, or how distressing the situation seemed, the old mule fought panic and just kept right on SHAKING IT OFF AND STEPPING UP!

TEN LIFE PRINCIPLES

It wasn't long before the old mule, battered and exhausted, stepped triumphantly over the wall of that well! What seemed like it would bury him actually helped him . . . all because of the manner in which he handled his adversity.

Even though the mule faced certain death at the beginning, instead of giving up, the mule created an opportunity to survive by changing its paradigm of the situation.

POSITIVE LIFE SKILLS AND TOOLS

"The starting point of all achievement is desire."
Napoleon Hill

Your Awakening

There's an old farmer who owns a large piece of land with a pond. Over the past forty years, he builds a beautiful beach and pagoda for his family and friends to enjoy.

One day he decides to go out to inspect the pond. As he walks along, he hears voices and laughter. As he gets closer he notices a bunch of women's clothing scattered about and realizes they are skinny-dipping.

One of the ladies notices the man and screams for him to leave. Not knowing who he was and why he was there, another woman yelled, "We're not coming out and letting you see us naked you disgusting old man" as the rest of the woman cheered in agreement.

They started to congregate towards the deep end of the pond. When the man yelled back, "Relax ladies. I didn't come here to stop you from swimming or to see you naked. I just came here to feed the alligator."

POSITIVE LIFE SKILLS AND TOOLS

It is time for you to wake up. It is time for you to stop hitting the snooze button on your alarm clock and sleeping through your life. Today's the day, now is the time, there's no better time to get started. There are alligators in the water and you don't even realize it.

An Invitation to the Feast

Imagine it's the medieval times and you've been invited by special invitation to a celebration and feast at the King's Castle. You've heard about these gatherings from others in town, but you've never been worthy enough to be included yourself. Well, today's the day. You are invited to not only come to the King's Castle, but expected to actually sit at the King's Table. The feast is about to begin, but you are the only guest remaining to arrive.

There will be all types of food, beverages, and desserts. More than you have ever witnessed in your entire life. It doesn't matter what you like to eat...it will be there. If you want pizza, chicken wings, ice cream, filet mignon-it will be there. And dancing? There will be more fun, dancing and singing than you can possibly imagine. You can eat what you want and leave what you don't. No one is going to make you eat anything you don't want to eat. You can decide what you want all on your own.

93

POSITIVE LIFE SKILLS AND TOOLS

This is the final element to attracting "feathers" into your life. In addition to the "Three Steps" and the "Life Principles" this section provides practical skills and tools that can be used to attract "feathers." This is the Feast. These are useful strategies that can serve as a new foundation for living. Just like the feast, pick and choose what you like. Regardless of your choice, each tool can help you manifest your goals and dreams. There is no "right" or "best" one. Use them all, a combination, or just one. Welcome to the Feast!

Paradigm Shift Exercise

The word 'paradigm' comes from the Greek "paradeigma," which means model, pattern, or example. A paradigm is a set of beliefs that illustrates the way a person perceives the world. Paradigms vary from person to person, yet are extremely influential elements within life.

An individual's "paradigm" is a useful tool. It navigates daily life decisions and helps filter the numerous amounts of information. However, rigid paradigms create blocks to achieving goals, by creating limitations. Learning how to create paradigm shifts offers an opportunity to learn how to get out of your own way.

1. Think of something you learned how to do that was difficult or challenging.

POSITIVE LIFE SKILLS AND TOOLS

2. What was your thinking before you learned how to do it?
3. What were you feeling before you learned how to do it?
4. What did it take to learn how to do it?
5. What obstacles did you overcome to do it?
6. What were your thoughts after you learned how to do it?
7. How did you feel after you learned how to do it?
8. What life lesson did you learn from that event?

Paradigm shifts often occur unexpectedly, but can also be created by past life experiences. Every challenge a person faces in the present can be connected to a past event. The opportunity that was created in the past, affords a person the chance to develop and implement a new paradigm in the present.

Personal Vision Board

A Personal Vision is defined as what you want to create of yourself and the world around you. What does your vision include? Making a vital change in an area such as health, technology, or the environment? Raising happy, well-adjusted children? Writing a book? Owning a business? Living on a beach? Running a Tiki Hut? Being healthy? Visiting every continent? Helping others

POSITIVE LIFE SKILLS AND TOOLS

with their spiritual development? What are you good at? What do you love to do? What aren't you good at now, but you'd like to be? All of these important questions are part of identifying your personal vision.

Use the questions below to think through and start to craft your vision. It's adapted from many sources and will prompt you to think and dream. Find a place without distractions. Answer as many of the questions as possible, and be honest with yourself. Then take those ideas and put them into visual context by creating a Vision Board to be placed in a location where you can view it daily. It becomes a focal point of your thoughts, a goal of your actions, and a result of your desires.

1. Things I enjoy doing.
2. Things that bring me happiness/joy.
3. The two best moments of my past week.
4. Three things I'd do if I won the lottery.
5. Issues/Causes I care deeply about.
6. Most important values.
7. Things I can do well.
8. Top five bucket list items.

Personal Purpose Statement

Your Personal Purpose is about you, not about what you do. You are a human being, not a human doing. Your Personal Purpose Statement explains

POSITIVE LIFE SKILLS AND TOOLS

why you exist–your reason for being. To live a meaningful and satisfying life, you need to define what is meaningful and satisfying to you. Your Personal Purpose allows you to get the most out of your life. It is used in tandem with your Vision Board. It helps you to stay motivated, inspired and focused. And it assists in making decisions. When you have a decision to make, the question becomes easy–either your choice will support you in fulfilling your purpose or it won't. This ensures that the decisions that you make will better serve you. Your purpose is like a compass that is always guiding you in the right direction towards your vision.

In discovering your purpose it is important to note that it is not a goal. It is not something that you can ever finish. It is more of a guiding principle that states what you want your life to be about. It is not about acquiring money, status, power or material goods. All of those things are important in their own way, but in themselves, they are not the driving forces in your life. Your Personal Purpose is much more an integral part of you. It is more about what you want to express, and less about what you want to acquire.

Step One - Using the skill of brainstorming, make a list of everything that you want in your life. Don't over think the items on the list. Allow the ideas to

POSITIVE LIFE SKILLS AND TOOLS

come freely and quickly. Focus on what you want to express, or do, and not on what you want to acquire. In addition notice the feelings that arise and include them in the list.

Step Two - Identify the values that are most important to you. Allow them to come to the surface whether you use them or not. Create a list of as many of them as possible.

Step Three - List at least five goals that you want to achieve within the next six to twelve months. Think of personal, professional, educational, social, and health goal. The more specific the better.

Step Four - Identify the biggest challenges/ obstacles you want to overcome. Whether they are small and specific in nature, or more global and universal, create a list that has stopped you from achieving what you really want.

Step Five - Review each of the four lists and narrow down the most significant/important one from each and circle it.

Step Six - Write your Purpose Statement by using the following statement-"I will (whatever you circled in Step 1), using my (whatever you circled in Step 2), to achieve (whatever you circled in Step 3) and in doing so will also overcome (whatever you circled in Step 4).

POSITIVE LIFE SKILLS AND TOOLS

Your Personal Purpose Statement is meant to be used as a focal point each day. Print it out and place it in locations where it will be visible to you.

SMART Goals

We all know that goals need to be "smart." However, most people do not set goals that are very smart, both literally and figuratively. They set goals that are not well thought out, or unattainable. A SMART Goal is not a literal goal, but rather an acronym that provides a greater opportunity for achievement. A person that understands the power of SMART Goals is ahead of the game. SMART stands for ~ Specific, Measurable, Achievable, Realistic, and Timeframe.

When setting goals, most people are not specific enough. For instance, a popular goal for many involves money. So they'll set a goal to be a millionaire, but that goal really isn't too specific. It may seem so, but there are numerous smaller goals that must be accomplished first before becoming a millionaire. The SMART Goal tool is actually more of a strategy than simply setting a goal. Each letter of the acronym involves a step that must be accomplished before a goal becomes a SMART Goal.

It is essential to be as *Specific* as possible-the more specific the better. It offers a greater chance

POSITIVE LIFE SKILLS AND TOOLS

of achievement. When you identify a goal, ask yourself "what is the first step?" For instance, using the example above about the goal of being a millionaire. It is important ask, "What is the first step to being a millionaire?" The answer may be to "save money." Ask again, "What is the first step to save money?" The answer may be, get a job. Ask again, "What is the first step to getting a job?" The answer may be, "Make a resume." And so on. If you can come up with a step, then your goal is not specific enough. Only after you can no longer think of a new step is your goal as specific as possible.

Next, once you have a goal create a way to **Measure** your success. Having a barometer creates a greater sense of accountability for the individual. Be very clear in your ability to demonstrate your measure of success. Think about how you would show someone that you accomplished your goal. Then ask yourself, is this goal **Achievable**? If it is great, if not, then it's not going to be a SMART Goal. If it is achievable, then ask, is it **Realistic**? Sometimes we have lofty goals that end up being unrealistic. However, if it passes this step, then you are set for the final step. What is the **Timeframe** needed to achieve the goal? Once a timeline is established and the other steps are fulfilled you now have a smart goal.

POSITIVE LIFE SKILLS AND TOOLS

The Amazing You

Several decades ago, there was a show on TV called the "Six Million Dollar Man." Steve Majors played the main character, Steve Austin. At the time, it was the most sophisticated special effects in television entertainment. Austin was an astronaut that severely injured himself upon impact during a rocket landing. He lost the use of one of his eyes, his right arm, and both of his legs. During the opening credits and montage, the voice over actor says, "We can rebuild him, bigger, stronger, faster." Then the famous music can be heard (na, na, na, na), with Steve Austin running faster, being stronger, and jumping higher. He is the six million dollar man.

Think about what it would be like to be amazing. What would it take for you to be amazing? What would you look like? What would you be? What would you have in your life? What skills would you want to have? What would it take for you to be that person? Use the following questions to help you create an "amazing" you.

Step One - Take the next three minutes and brainstorm ideas to help identify the main characteristics, qualities, skills, etc that would make you amazing. Regardless of whether or not you utilize these skills at this time, allow yourself to

4

POSITIVE LIFE SKILLS AND TOOLS

develop a list of ideas that would create the best "you."

Step Two - Review the list and select the top ten items in the group. Rewrite them into a second list.

Step Three - Look at each item on the second list and rate yourself on a scale of one to five, one being low and five being high. Evaluate yourself on how happy/satisfied/well you are able to accomplish that item.

Step Four - Select the top five characteristics/ qualities and write them down into a third list. However, this time, write down some type of action that you must take to move up on the scale one number. Be sure to make that action item something that can actually be accomplished by you.

Now you have an action plan of your top five characteristics/qualities that can make you "amazing." Use the SMART Goals process and start your plan today.

Smiles

I once heard that a smile generates "one of the most positive emotional reactions." Smiling stimulates the brain's reward mechanisms. Energy signals travel throughout the brain engaging the "smiling" muscles. Once the muscles in the face

POSITIVE LIFE SKILLS AND TOOLS

contract, a positive feedback loop returns to the brain and reinforces the feeling of joy.

Smiles are generally divided into two categories-standard and genuine. A standard smile uses the muscles surrounding the mouth (think of "smile for the camera"), while the genuine utilizes both the muscles around the mouth and eyes (an instantaneous smile caused by a reaction to something positive).

A 2012 study by psychologists Tara Kraft and Sarah Pressman[15] suggests smiling reduces stress throughout the body and mind. They generate positive emotions. That's why people often feel happier around children–they smile more. On average, a child smiles 400 times a day. While happy people still smile 40-50 times a day, the average adult only does so 20 times.

Smiling is easy. Start by making a list of all the things that make you smile. Then identify the five top things that make you smile the most. Now, take one of the top five things that make you smile and articulate in great detail why.

1. What is the specific activity-use as many adjectives as possible?
2. With whom does this activity take place?
3. What type of day/year?
4. Before or after what?

POSITIVE LIFE SKILLS AND TOOLS

There are more you can include, but hopefully you get the picture. By fully articulating the event, situation, or activity, you are making it much more real and exciting. As a result, you are much more likely to go do more of it because it resonates. It is amazing.

Now, can you imagine what your life would be like if you spent every waking hour only doing things on that list? Not possible, you say? Wrong. You can do it. So who would you have to be to simply be and do your 100 Smiles list? What commitments would you need to make? What changes would be necessary and appropriate?

Free Hugs

During a recent vacation, I was walking around an amusement park with my family when my wife and I saw two people wearing "Free Hugs" t-shirts. We let out a shriek, ran over to them, and asked if we could have a "free hug." Our kids thought we were a bit crazy, but alas we received our free hug-not only one, but two (one from each person). We thanked them and went on our way to the next ride.

Hugs are amazing. There is an undeniable power of a hug. It offers a wonderful form of giving love to those around you and those who are near. They build strong bonds with the people you see everyday, cultivating trust, increasing confidence

POSITIVE LIFE SKILLS AND TOOLS

and making us happier. Hugging also induces oxytocin which has the ability to stimulate solidarity between strangers. In addition, a good hug lowers stress and blood pressure and reconnects the mind with the body. A hug is one of the easiest ways to acknowledge another person's importance.

Become a hugger today. Go in with intent. Go heart to heart. Show someone they matter.

"SW" Rule

When it comes to facing failure, mistakes and challenges it is often best to invoke the "Rule of So What." It is a relatively easy way to address a situation instead of getting angry, upset and frustrated. Remember failure is not something you become. It is an event, not a determination of who you are as a person.

The SW Rule states: *"Some Will, Some Won't, So What, Someone or Something else is Waiting."* For example, your goal might be to get a particular client's business. You do everything correctly. You set up a meeting, have a great sales pitch, get great feedback, but they choose another vendor. Sure you can get upset, who wouldn't? Instead of complaining, or trying to come up with possible reasons, say out loud, "So What!" It is important to realize that you are not going to close every deal or even move every potential prospect to the next

POSITIVE LIFE SKILLS AND TOOLS

step. That does not make you a failure. In fact, it is this step that you can learn from. Some clients Will sign; Some clients Won't; So What; Someone else is Waiting!

Learn from the experience and move on to the next. From this point forward when you feel like you failed, take a look back and review what happened. There is a learning point in that event. Learn, make yourself better and move on, as there are others looking for what you have to offer.

CONCLUSION

"We don't beat the reaper by living longer, we beat the reaper by living well and living fully."
Randy Pausch

So now what? Where do you go from here? Where do you start? Are you all talk, but no action? Or, are you ready to step up and move forward?

In **Chapter One** the concept of the Law of Attraction was introduced to create the proper mindset. The Law of Attraction may not be "proved" through a scientific formula, but it does exist whether you "believe" it or not.

In **Chapter Two** you learned a *Three Step* formula that can be implemented immediately. It is a powerful strategy that supports any form of success or goal you want to achieve. The more familiar you become with them, the easier they are to develop. Positive people have successful habits. The *Three Steps* are designed to create a positive routine towards your goals. However, beware of *The Big Three*. The little voices in your head that get in your way. Your *Parrot, Limiting Beliefs, and Perception (PLP)* are going to speak loudly when you first begin. It is their role to keep you right where you are, in your comfort zone. Acknowledge them, validate them, but choose not to listen to them. Thank them for "protecting you." But, maximize their energy to turn challenges into opportunities.

107

CONCLUSION

In **Chapter Three**, ten principles are shared to enhance your current life blueprint. Commit these ideas to memory by repeating them daily. Look for opportunities in your actions each day that align with these principles. Perhaps, select one principle each week, and practice using them in your routines. Thoughts lead to feelings, feelings lead to actions, actions lead to results. If you don't like your results, change your beliefs. As they root themselves into your mind, you will find yourself looking at life through different lenses. From there you will begin to make new choices creating new results.

In **Chapter Four**, various exercises and tools are presented. These skills are imperative for change to be permanent. In addition to the *Three Steps* and *Ten Principles*, you must put all the material shared into practice. Don't just read about them, think about them, or talk about them. Commit to a plan today. Don't say, "I don't have time" or "these won't work for me." Whether you purchased this book on your own, or it was a gift, you "attracted" it. Do the exercises, and watch drastic changes in your life.

Let's Play a Game

There are many life lessons that can be learned by playing games. One of the most popular boardgames of all time is Monopoly. The earliest known version, "The Landlords Game" was created

CONCLUSION

in 1904 by Lizzie Magie. She designed it to illustrate economics and teach about rent, land, privilege and taxation. After losing his job following the Stock Market Crash of 1929, Charles Darrow created his own version called Monopoly. His game was designed to inform people about real estate, land ownership, and how to create wealth. After a failed attempt to sell the game, some revisions, and self-marketing, he sold it to Parker Brothers as the games inventor. What began as an educational tool became an international phenomenon with numerous editions, world-wide tournaments, digital versions, and a brand that stands alone.

Baseball is another game that teaches numerous lessons. There is no other team sport like it. Sport experts agree that the skills required to play baseball are some of the most difficult to perfect within athletics. The odds of hitting a ball that is thrown only sixty feet-six inches from the point of contact, by a person holding a wooden stick is astronomical. The professionals involved that can hit that ball and put it in play are only effective thirty (30) percent of the time. The other seventy (70) percent end in disappointment. What other profession would ever allow an employee to succeed with that ratio? Consider the principle shared earlier about challenges and how that relates to this great game.

CONCLUSION

"Feathers are Everywhere" is both a literal and figurative title. As demonstrated, all a person needs to do is open their eyes and see that feathers are indeed all around. So, the hunt for feathers begins now. Throughout this book there are feathers scattered amongst the pages. Some are obvious, some hide in plain sight, while others seem to blend in and get lost. Count the number of feathers and send me an email with the number you counted to CoachRandy@CoachRandySays.com. Those that get it correct will receive a special gift that can be used to help manifest your goals and dreams, along with a complimentary coaching session on any aspect of the book. Those that don't...well you will still receive a little something for the effort. So there's nothing to loose by counting the feathers... they are everywhere.

For additional resources, tools and questions be sure to visit **www.FeathersAreEverywhere.com**. There you will find:

- Additional information about the book
- A printable Three Step worksheet
- A printable list of the Ten Life Principles
- Additional resources
- Various presentations around "Feathers" and the Law of Attraction
- Future webinar/seminar dates for those that want to learn more about the LOA.

RESOURCE GUIDE

1 - *"Think and Grow Rich"* is one of the first personal development and self-improvement books ever written. It was authored by Napoleon Hill and published in 1937. He was inspired by a suggestion from business magnate Andrew Carnegie. He wanted to help people in all lines of work attain wealth and achieve success. Hill wrote the book during the Great Depression with over 70 million copies worldwide being sold through 2015. Hill studied the characteristics of successful people and introduces the 13 principles for personal success.

2 - *"Inside Out"* is a 2015 animated film produced by Pixar Animation Studios and released by Walt Disney Pictures. It was directed and co-written by Pete Docter. The film is set in the mind of a young girl, 11 year-old Riley Andersen, where the emotions of Joy, Sadness, Fear, Anger, and Disgust lead her through life as her parents move the family from Minnesota to San Francisco. Throughout the story we come to appreciate the importance of each emotion, even though some create discomfort and possible pain.

3 - *"Millennial Minds: The Worried Well"* is and online survey of 3,530 teens and adults, including 2,015 adult millennials by Allidura Consumer, GSW Health, and the Harris Poll. They focused on the big tension of millennials between their aspirations for happiness (97% say it's important) and the way

they are currently living: more stressed, anxious and depressed than any other living generation.

4 - *"Man's Search for Meaning,"* written by Viktor Frankl chronicles his experiences as an inmate in Auschwitz concentration camp during World War II. The book focuses on the early day concept of mindset facing the most difficult of life's experiences. Frankl concludes that meaning can be found in every moment of living. Life never ceases to have meaning, even in suffering loss and facing death. It is up to the individual's perception and their freedom of choice do decide the meaning.

5 - *"Law of Attraction: The Science of Attracting More of What You Want and Less of What you Don't Want,"* written by Michael Losier is currently one on of the most popular books about the Law of Attraction. Following the lead of Esther and Jerry Hicks, his book provides an easy-to-follow three step formula focusing on energy and vibrations. He is a Canadian Law of Attraction teacher and author of numerous books. You can join his weekly learning "Hang out with Michael" where he provides handouts, worksheets and other tools. You can join him at www.hangoutwithmichael.com

6 - *"Ask and it is Given,"* by Esther and Jerry Hicks is a book about the teachings of the nonphysical entity Abraham. Esther dialogs with a group of spiritual teachers who call themselves Abraham.

RESOURCE GUIDE

From these conversations she is able to address well-being, joy, and help others achieve all that is desired in life. In 1986, the "Abraham Tapes" were recorded beginning an unexpected journey working with tens of thousands of people. The messages on the tapes provide numerous lessons and have been used and documented throughout the world. Esther and Jerry are one of the first to address LOA and teach it to the masses. Esther Hicks served as a primary inspiration for the national phenomenon "The Secret."

7 - *"The Secret"* is a film (then book 2006) by Australian writer and producer, Rhonda Bryne. It is based on the Law of Attraction where positive thinking can create life-changing results such as increased happiness, health, and wealth. Over 19 million copies have been sold and translated into more than 40 languages. She introduces a three-step process for achieving goals-ask, believe, and receive; based on a quote from the Bible "And all things, whatsoever ye shall ask in prayer, believing, ye shall receive." (Matthew 21:22) In addition, she highlights gratitude and visualization as the two most powerful skills to achieve success.

8 - *"Secrets of the Millionaire Mind"* published by Harper Collins in 2005 is from author, businessman and motivational speaker T. Harv Eker. The book focuses on the mindset of wealthy individuals and a

RESOURCE GUIDE

collection of "mental attitudes that facilitate wealth." Eker claims we each possess a "financial blueprint," or an "internal script that dictates how we relate to money." By changing this blueprint people can change their ability to accumulate wealth. He lists seventeen ways rich people differ from middle class and the poor. You can attend a Millionaire Mind Intensive (MMI) training at www.millionairemindbook.com

9 - *"The Four Agreements"* published in 1997 was written by Mexican author and Toltec spiritualist, Don Miguel Ruiz. The book advocates personal freedom from internal agreements that we have made with ourselves and others that create obstacles and limited happiness in our lives.

10 - *"Mindset: The New Psychology of Success"* was written by world-renowned Stanford University psychologist Carol Dweck. Through her decades of research on achievement and success she discovered the power of our mindset. Dweck explains why it's not just our abilities and talent that bring us success—but whether we approach them with a fixed or growth mindset.

11 - *"Don't Give Up"* was an acceptance speech delivered on March 4, 1993, by Jim Valvano. He was awarded the inaugural Arthur Ashe Courage and Humanitarian Award at the first-ever ESPY Awards. Despite being weakened from his fight

against cancer, he delivered an energetic and inspiring speech that brought the crowd to its feet.

12 - *"The Soul of Money,"* (2003) by Lynne Twist examines attitudes toward money–how it is earned, spent, invested, and given away. Using powerful stories and practical principles, paradigm shifts are created around the feelings of scarcity and guilt with sufficiency and freedom.

13 - *"The Dash"* was written in 1996 by Linda Ellis. She drew her inspiration while working in a stressful and tense work environment. This poem has impacted millions and millions of people.

14 - *"Pain-Pleasure Principle"* was the foundation of Dr. Sigmund Freud's psychoanalytic theory of personality. The pleasure principle is the driving force that seeks immediate gratification of all needs, wants, and urges. The pain-pleasure principle lies at the core of everything you do, and of everything you are. Your beliefs, values and psychological rules are all built upon this principle.

15 - *"Grin and Bear It! Smiling Facilitates Stress Recovery"* Psychological scientists Tara Kraft and Sarah Pressman of the University of Kansas in 2012 investigated the potential benefits of smiling by looking at how different types of smiling, and the awareness of smiling, affects individuals' ability to recover from episodes of stress.

RESOURCE GUIDE

Famous People & LOA

Oprah Winfrey
(Actress/Entrepreneur/Philanthropist)

In 1984, prior to being in the movie The Color Purple, Oprah was consumed with the story. She purchased the book for all her friends and thought about it constantly. When she moved to Chicago, she got a call from a casting director to be in her first movie. It turned out to be a role in "The Color Purple."

Arnold Schwarzenegger
(Actor/Former California Governor)

Before Arnold was a huge movie star, he was a body builder. When he said he wanted to be an action movie actor no one believed him. People said his last name was too hard to pronounce and his accent was too difficult to understand. However, he didn't care what other said and knew what he wanted to be even if no one else did. Using the same focus to become Mr. Olympia, he used the same amount of energy towards his acting career. He became one of the largest movie stars in Hollywood...even the governor of California.

Jim Carrey
(Comedian/Actor)

Prior to becoming famous, Jim Carey spent a lot of time in his car. At one point he was homeless and had no other place to live. He often drove to Muholland Drive in Los Angeles visualizing producers and directors working with him. This was part of his daily routine. He even wrote himself a $10,000,000 check for "Acting Services Rendered" that he kept in his wallet. On Thanksgiving in 1995 he was paid $10,000,000 for Dumb And Dumber.

Redfoo
(Musician/Entertainer)

Redfoo is part of LMFAO and was featured in the song "Duet" in the 1998 Black Eyed Peas album. He loved hip hop and wanted to be a success in the music business. He realized the power of positivity using his lyrics to attract his ambitions. The Black Eyed Peas also sang about the things they wanted focusing on the positive. LMFAO's lyrics in "Yes" says, "every day I see my dream" all throughout the song.

RESOURCE GUIDE

Fun Games About LOA

"I Spy" ~

Decide on something you want to see. Pick one thing. It can be anything. For example: I want to see a boy in a baseball hat, or I want to see a yellow car. You then set the intention that you will see it that day. At the end of the day, share what you saw or write it down.

Attitude of Gratitude ~

Gratitude is one of the highest forms of positive energy. Our feelings of gratitude attract into our lives more of those things that we appreciate.

Place a rubber band around your wrist. Tell yourself that every time you look at the band you are going to think of one thing that makes you grateful. As you express gratitude, more things will show up in your life for which you feel grateful.

Wish Keeper ~

Write down all your wishes, dreams or goals onto small pieces of paper. Then place them into a box, container, vase and let them work their magic.

ACKNOWLEDGEMENTS

The idea behind this book was developed a number of years ago, but the chapters within were written in a few months time. Only after my two youngest daughters, Mikayla and Brianna, kept after me asking when the book was going to be finished did I even begin to write. Over a six month period this book has changed, evolved and adapted to the currents in life's stream. It is very likely it will continue to grow as change is constant.

Anyone who has ever authored a book knows the hardest part is not in the writing, not even in the publishing, but rather in the selling. There is nothing more difficult than encouraging strangers to invest a few dollars to buy your book. If this book is in your hands either by the generosity of a purchase, or it was gifted to you, I want to say, 'thank you.' I appreciate the time you will take to read the words, listen to the message, and hopefully implement the "Three Steps." Frankly, finishing the book is merely the beginning. Using the principles, engaging the steps, and utilizing the tools are really what it will take to notice the feathers.

My kids and I play a game on a regular basis. By now they are conditioned. But, whenever I see a feather I point to it and say, "Hey, what's that?" Of course they respond, "A feather." Then I ask, "What do we know about feathers?" They roll their eyes and say, "Yeah Dad, we know, they are

ACKNOWLEDGEMENTS

everywhere." Now they even spot feathers on their own letting me know when they saw one during their day. So here's the secret, this book is really for them. It's my blueprint to help them navigate the journey within their own life. A core responsibility of any parent is to prepare their child(ren) to live independently. My oldest daughter and son stopped listening to my advice years ago. However, my two youngest are still somewhat impressionable. I figure by writing a book like this, they will be more inclined to learn these lessons by reading what I want them to know, than listening to me. I want them to understand what is shared from my heart to theirs in hopes someday they too will realize that all of their dreams can be achieved. The Law of Attraction is present in their lives, and they have the power to manifest whatever they turn their attention to.

To my Angel, the wings on which I fly. You are my everything of every day and every moment. You are the most important person in my life. I am so fortunate that our souls found one another and they continue to dance together in perfect harmony. There is no doubt the Law Of Attraction brought you to me-it is proof it works! Thank you for being my number one advocate, editor, publicist, muse, best friend, and mother of my children.

ACKNOWLEDGEMENTS

To my many clients and students who have heard me teach (and at times preach) the message within these pages time again during our coaching sessions. Sometimes it made complete sense, while at other times it seemed like it was impossible to comprehend. You continued to open yourself and focus to engage in the learning process.

The universe brought "feathers" to me during an important transition in my life. Only after I quit my career in 2005 was I able to understand the power of the Law of Attraction. Thank you to Bruce Schneider and the iPEC community for being instrumental in that transformation.

I have been blessed with a network of incredible professionals, mentors, friends and heroes in my life. Thank you to Tom Rebyak, Gary Berger, Noam Kritzer, Jeff Dunst, Mark Risenberg, Sam Hart, Michelle and Adam Shandler, Rabbi Randi Mustnitsky and Rabbi Ron Kaplan, Jonah Kaplan, Rafe Kaplan, Josh Rosen, Susan Werk, Rabbi Alan Silverstein, Lee Rosenfield, and Jim Thompson and my friends and colleagues with the Positive Coaching Alliance. Our meetings, conversations, partnerships, and opportunities continue to flood my life with compassion, love and support.

121

ABOUT THE AUTHOR

Randy Nathan (aka Coach Randy) has worked with thousands of individuals to help create better lives. He is the President/CEO of Project NextGen a leadership, training, and professional coaching organization. Having earned his BA from the University of Colorado (Sociology & Education), an MSW from the University of Southern California, an MA in Executive Non-Profit Management from Hebrew Union College, and his coaching certification from iPEC Coaching, Randy has spent over twenty-five years inspiring individuals as a motivational speaker, edutainer, athletic coach, adjunct professor, camp director, professional coach, and author. He has partnered with professionals throughout the world by inspiring and motivating them to achieve their personal goals and dreams, while teaching them valuable strategies to overcome the obstacles and challenges they encounter.

Coach Randy is also a renown expert on the Millennial Generation (individuals born between 1980-2001) and national Anti-Bullying Advocate. He is the Creator of The Power of PRIDE, the LEAP Program, Student Leadership Academy, College with PURPOSE, Career JumpStart, Workforce 2.0 and Peak Performance Coaching – empowerment programs designed to help individuals identify their purpose, overcome limiting beliefs, enhance relationships, and develop a plan for reaching their

ABOUT THE AUTHOR

true potential. As a Sports Bully Expert he has worked with countless individuals who have been bullied, as well as those who bully. He is part of a national movement to reinvent a more positive experience within youth sports. His first book, "Bullying in Sports: A Guide to Identifying the Injuries We Don't See" is available online at www.BullyingInSports.com.

For additional resources, tools and questions be sure to visit www.FeathersAreEverywhere.com.

Coach Randy provides keynote presentations and trainings on a number of topics including leadership, success, happiness, bullying in sports, team building, anti-bullying, mental preparation, motivation and other pertinent issues. Visit his speaking website at www.CoachRandySays.com. He is looking for collaborative partners as well as opportunities to engage in healthy growth. You can also follow him on Twitter @CoachRandySays, facebook.com/coachrandysays, youtube/coachrandysays, and linkedin.com/coachrandy.

Randy Nathan resides in New Jersey along with his wife and four children.